The DNA of a Winner

The DNA of a Winner

8 Steps to Building the Soulprint of a Winner

Brad Dalton

Published by Game Changer Publishing

ISBN: 978-1-7365491-4-8

www.PublishABestSellingBook.com

DEDICATION

This book has been a work in progress on the Success Road for as long as I can remember and is dedicated to my chief encouragement team. Cori, Cooper, and Bronco.... Thank you for bringing the right balance of crazy, fun, and discipline to our lives.

DEDICATION

This book has been a work in progress on the Success Road for as long as I can remember and is dedicated to my chief encouragement team. Cori, Cooper, and Bronco.... Thank you for bringing the right balance of crazy, fun, and discipline to our lives.

DOWNLOAD YOUR FREE GIFTS

Read This First

Just to say thanks for buying and reading my book, I would like to give you a 100% bonus gift for FREE, no strings attached!

To Download Now, Visit:

www.BradDaltonGroup.com/freegift

The DNA of a Winner

8 Steps to Building the Soulprint of a Winner

Brad Dalton

www.PublishABestSellingBook.com

Acknowledgments

What an experience it is has been leading to the publication of this book. I am forever grateful for those who have weathered the storm with me and experienced with me the feeling of being fed with a fire hose while writing this book. There are so many different individuals who had an influence and played a key role in making this book what it is.

Thank you, Cris Cawley, for being the ultimate leader, friend, and support staff. You are the glue to the operation and fantastic at what you do.

Thank you, Game Changer Publishing staff, for providing a platform specific to individuals looking to not only make a difference but leave a positive imprint on others.

Thank you, Rachel Ryden, Jen Prater, Erin Boyle, Penni Allen, and Denise Knight, for your positively infectious attitudes and brainstorming at the roots of this journey.

Thank you, Mom, Dad, Zac, JD, Tracye, and Ricky, for your love and support. Family is the bedrock for all who I am, and I've got a great base!

Thank you, Mike, Anita, Scott, Haylee, Boone, Ora Gay, Ed "Too Tall" Freeman, and Barbara, for allowing me to walk into your lives and welcome me with open arms. Your compassion is unmatched.

Thank you, Stephanie Fornander, Sondra Lavoie, and Aisa Jenkins, for your friendship and positive vibrations throughout the journey. There is power to positive!

Thank you, Dr. Larry Rogien, for inspiring me years ago to be an educator and showing me the value of authentic, inspired teachings. I went from a guy wanting to teach so I could coach to a guy who wanted to teach and also coach. You were a game changer.

Thank you, Kathryn Wayne, for showing genuine interest in me as a student many years ago. You inspired me to read, write, and be the best version of myself. You are one of the most influential figures in my teaching career, and needless to say, your style zinged with my style of learning!

Thank you, Sherm and Nancy Button, for putting students first and being a source of inspiration for so many in your time as educators.

Thank you to all educators out there trying to make a massive impact in kids' lives despite extraordinary circumstances. You are my heroes and sheroes!

Thank you, Jake Taylor and Rick Baumann, two great baseball coaches and great friends but, more importantly, two men of positive influence for many young adults.

Thank you, Jon Gordon, Brendan Kane, Sheri Riley, Samantha Kris, Shannon Rose Farrell-Jackson, Michelle Lewis, Kirt Manecke, CJ Beatty, Zach Brandon, Viliami Tuivai, Heather Chauvin, Thane Marcus Ringler, Patrick Fitzgibbons, Andrew Kap, Beth Miller, Greg Hahn, Bernadett Nagy, Anna McAfee, Ben Ward, Danny Shannon, Zenas Chin, Steve Fifta, Manny Lavery, Jennifer King, Ryan McCarty, Ryan Lockard, Dr. Kaleb Redden, Tim Davis, Dr. Jim Van Allan, and Edna III for your time on the Best Self Podcast and your dedication to adding value to the lives of others.

Thank you, Paul Chehey, for being the positive influence when I needed to pivot my priorities and career trajectory. Your impact is far-reaching, and if the world's roster were full of Paul Chehey's, it would be STRONG! MIAGO!

Thank you, Hanke Kvamme, for being a great friend and a positive warrior for anybody lucky enough to be in your circle.

Thank you to my students. You're the juice that keeps me moving down the success road. I'm forever grateful for having had the opportunity to build relationships and shape culture with you.

Table of Contents

Introduction

A gift has been handed to you, one that has the power to choose and change your path through life. You were created as an unrepeatable miracle, and this world was made for you to experience unprecedented success. Today the sun came up. It met the horizon and then rose above it. It raced at roughly 1000 mph from the east as we spun, yet many of us stand around like time is waiting for us. Somewhere along the line, many have become complacent and stopped being impressed or interested. Many have begun to see the world in monochrome, but this does not change the fact that all the brilliant colors that make up the earth were painted for your eyes. Get ready to push past your limitations and experience the success, love, joy, growth, income, and the ability to positively impact all who come in contact with you. Are you ready to go full out and claim your birthright of excellence?

Imagine for a moment what your life would look like next year if you could radically and positively transform every aspect of your life...

... your relationships...

... your mental hygiene...

... your ascending career trajectory...

... your finances...

... your physical health...

... your levels of enjoyment and fun...

... even your level of contribution to your community...

You are enough....... your journey is waiting for you.

There are ways in which emotions help shape your life, like those deep feelings of euphoria in your gut, those toe-curling goosebump causing moments, and even the sinking feeling of fear that sometimes makes you feel like your heart is about to burst; all of these emotions have conceivably helped you retain information and have had a dramatic influence on your dynamic present and future.

Questions are an inevitable part of your journey through life; they are a means through which you can judge and evaluate yourself, so as you go, here are some that you should have in mind.

- Am I living the type of life that I believe I was meant to live and deserve?
- Are my eyes yet open?
- How does an individual denied a VISA eight times, grinding away with a Silicon Valley communication startup, turn a daydream into a global communications giant?

- How does a college dropout go from a sports science major to moving to the Himalayas to creating a mindfulness app that serves 30 plus million users worldwide?
- How does Santo Domingo of the Dominican Republic produce the fourth-highest percentage of professional baseball talent in the world?

I have always held leadership positions for as long as I can remember. I am a lifelong educator; I was a head coach for many years, and I can tell you without an iota of doubt that we all have that unique LeBron type of gift or talent within our own dynamic radius. We all have our own version of Vishen Lakhiani, Steve Jobs, or Mark Zuckerberg talent within us. Inside the DNA of a Winner, like a banana, we peel back layers of what produces these types of winning rosters, winning teams, winning workplaces, and winning individuals. In all of the cases above, individuals are writing their dreams down, eating the dream, sleeping the dream, talking about the dream, and accomplishing the dream starting not on the pedestal but at square one. Starting small and targeting the best versions of themselves.

If you could pinpoint one moment in time where the hair on your arms stood up, what would it be? Feel it. See it. Wholeheartedly immerse yourself in it again.

Can you remember a point in your life where you felt so euphoric that you thought you would pass out? Visualize how you felt and what made you feel that way, find it and immerse yourself in it again. You are good enough, smart enough, and deserving enough to live a life that causes the hair on your skin to rise while competing and performing tasks that you are passionate about.

NOW IS THAT TIME

You are writing your story, every action you take, every move you make is a chapter in the book of your life. When you are no longer here, and your book is read aloud to all those who will come after, what do you want them to say about you? Your company and/or team can bridge the gap between high potential and high performance, and all can be put in motion within the next 30 seconds. It's worth noting that all the feelings you have experienced in your brightest and even darkest moments are part of what makes you. Those emotions are the language of your heart. They separate you from everyone else. It is never enough to merely listen to the words that other people speak. You must always listen to your heart because sometimes, the truth is hidden just beneath the surface, and only your mind's eye can see it. We create evergreen moments and love-based space from the inside out. Champions in life are those who choose to let their confidence conquer doubt, openly welcome disruption, rely on their concentrated focus to defeat distractions, and have the ability to choose the right attitude. By enhancing mental acuity and buying into loved based thinking, you realize your mind can either be your worst enemy or a potential performance edge. The nuggets gifted in this book will always help you improve the previous best versions of yourself and become a more confident, tough-minded optimist.

Mental mapping is often talked about but too often ignored. The majority of focus in school, in the workplace, and/or on the field is placed on the mechanical process, leaving the mental game to chance. The thought process involved in being a confident and self-aware person is a difficult and dedicated effort that must be practiced and perfected over time. The benefit of buying into the idea of gaining a mental edge is that when you finally do, positive changes tend to happen relatively quickly. Let the material in this book help develop your ability to prepare, cope, overcome adversity, create self-awareness, build your brand, shape a lifestyle, and bridge the gap between potential and performance in life. Those with the DNA of a champion put their minds in a position to be successful. Success breeds confidence, and confidence helps your best self thrive.

For this book to help you, it needs your permission. As you read, it is your responsibility to weave this material into your life and let it become a part of your DNA. You will be asked to unpack and sort through some principles that you have about life. You will have to discard those that do not align with a champion's mindset and adopt new ones that do. As it is in life, you'll only get out of it what you put into it. If you will take pride in preparation, hard work, studying your craft, and being the best you can be, within reason, there is nothing in life you cannot accomplish. Prepare to Succeed.

CHAPTER 1

Attitude

Stay out of the weeds, feed the P's

Highly Successful Thinkers Know Nothing

Everyone is an exceptional being with a unique talent that only they can share with the world. However, the difference between those who achieve their potential and those who don't is that the former understands that they still have so much to learn.

I remember feeling so sure about myself as a young adult, believing that I had so many answers and such a great sense of self. I can also remember being at my lowest point, questioning myself and feeling lost, wondering if I had what it took. Five years later, I realized that I didn't have the grip on success that I thought I did. Ten years later, I learned I had so much more to learn than I previously thought. In the end, you must realize that the secret sauce is your attitude. In my case, I had to confront myself and say, "You are not going to do me like this anymore." I was not going to let my mindset sabotage me. I was going to choose the right attitude, and you will need to do the same. Say it out loud, "you will not do me like this anymore." Your attitude is what you crawl out of bed with, dive into every day with, and hit the pillow with each night as you go to sleep. Growth, intentional thinking, culture shaping, becoming your best self, the double win, etc., all begin with choosing the right attitude. Can I get an amen to choosing the right attitude? Are you done giving yourself a pass and ready to live abundantly?

A "stand tall" mentality and a thankful awareness are necessary as you weave your way through life despite all the challenges handed down to you. As you examine your thought process and all the other parts of your life, don't forget to examine the attitude with which you face life. Having the right attitude and mindset is an integral part of being a winner. The type of reaction you let people or situations provoke out of you will determine whether you are in control or are being controlled. A champion is always in control. Choose to always have a positive mindset and outlook on life. The ability to recognize negative thoughts and immediately transform them into positive thoughts is a crucial part of being a winner. Champions are those kinds of people others always want to work with, those who everyone wants on their team because they know that the work will be smooth, enjoyable, and efficient with them.

Sometimes you must sit and allow life to slow down around you, get some perspective, master your emotions, and find the best ways to be in control of them. When you do this, it becomes easier to recognize your stressors and switch your negative feelings to positive ones. As you do this, fulfillment begins to replace and dominate the fear in your heart. Empowerment becomes your culture. A lifestyle riddled with negative thoughts creates a circle of constant discrediting and underestimation of yourself. All this work begins in your mind before it is manifested in the physical. Many times, it isn't that you can't create a better version of you; it's that your previous life is holding you hostage. That person two weeks ago, two months ago, two years ago is holding you hostage. Confront you and let yourself know that this will no longer be an option. Sometimes the only variable that needs to change is the conversation with yourself.

Attitude equals dignity; attitude is valor, power, confidence, honesty, and integrity. Self-aware human beings:

- Control their attitude.
- Form a controllable plan about what to do.
- Focus and trust that approach one day at a time.
- Choose to stay in a positive mindset where they recognize big feelings and switch them back to positive–this is huge.

To create and maintain a healthy, liberating lifestyle in an ever-changing 3-second world (social media), the work must begin within the mind. Attitude is what teaches us to walk tall. It is not an attitude of arrogance but rather a mindset of pride and self-worth–a mindset that places value on effort, not achievement.

Self-Worth is based on effort, not achievement.

Effort

Think of yourself trying to bake a cake for the first time. You must have a picture already of what you expect that cake to look like when you are done, but you cannot wish it into existence. You have to work to bring that cake to life. The effort is that work, mixing the ingredients that make the cake, making sure that all of them are in the right proportions, setting the oven, and watching until the cake is baked. All these are what I mean by effort. As in real life, even after you have done your best to make sure that the cake comes out perfect, you may not get it right on the first trial. You might have to try again and again before you get something even remotely identical to the picture in your head. Getting that perfect cake will not be easy, but if you are resilient and keep trying, you will finally succeed, and when you do, nobody can take away from you the experience and confidence gained through that process.

Effort is a controllable factor. Do not tie your value as a person to your ability to win competitions, win promotions, or excel better than others; instead, you should put stock into yourself because you are a human being deserving of all the good that life has to offer. Place value on family and friends and your relationships with your coworkers, teammates, and others. Let your integrity be one of the reasons why others value you. Let them see the effort you put into positively impacting their lives instead of you trying to compete with them. Anyone who adds value to others' lives will draw people to themselves, while those who devalue will force people to withdraw from them.

In your journey to becoming your best self, the only competition that matters most is the one between who you were, who you are, and who you are trying to be. The effort is about you versus you. You are the only one that knows your true limits; you know when you are giving a hundred percent and doing your best. It is necessary to note that doing your best does not mean overstretching yourself and being something you're not. If the best you can do is a seven out of ten that day, give one hundred percent of that seven.

As I stated earlier, everybody has the LeBron talent within their own dynamic radius. Everybody has a Lionel Messi gift, tailored perfectly to suit their skillset and sphere of influence. If you cannot trap a ball, hold a pen. If you cannot hold a pen, hold a paintbrush, a microphone, or even a chisel. Whatever your gifts or talents are, take charge of them and dominate. All you need is already within you; you just have to find it and hone it until it becomes something you don't need to think too much about to excel at. Find that talent, shave out the fluff, seal the leaks, and watch yourself soar. Shaving the fluff out of your attitude and effort and tapping into what is already in your tank is an attainable task. Your IQ, athletic abilities, or inabilities are not the only things that matter in your journey through life. Those things give you an advantage, but they do not guarantee your success. We can all be better versions of ourselves, whether we possess those talents/ skills or not, the DNA of champions does not discriminate, and it runs in your veins. You, me, and we can all be better versions of ourselves. No matter where you came from, your dreams are real, valid, and attainable!

When you think like a winner and play the part of a winner long enough, those positive affirmations, habits, and routines become a part of you and begin to bear fruit in your life. Your current location does not matter, the type of car you are driving does not matter either, your account balance is not a determinant; what matters is whether you are ready and willing to put in the work and be a forward-minded thinker. It might be a long road, but as long as your eyes aren't being deceived and you have bought into the right lens, you will surely reach a life of fulfillment. Are you ready?

Keys to Choosing the Right Attitude that makes good teams great.

If, as a driver, you get into your car every day, with nothing else on your mind but the fear of the bumps on the road, the possibility of accidents, or your car developing some kind of fault along the way, one day, you will decide not to get into that car anymore. Your fear will win. Fear of road bumps will only hinder your progress. You must understand that as you start to implement these principles into your life, you have automatically signed up for those things that will hinder you on the way. Don't avoid disruption. Embrace it. Embrace the obstacles you will meet on the road, embrace the inconveniences. As you do this, you also embrace the vibrations that will stimulate growth in your quest to be a difference-maker and an attitude shaper for others. Goals are sexy, and milestones are rewarding, but it's the disruption and the inconvenience that helps you climb higher mountains, conquer your greatest fears and get your biggest rewards.

Keys to maintaining a winning attitude:

1.) You've never reached *it*.

Don't ever get to a point where you feel like you have arrived. Never be so comfortable that you become stale and plateau in growth. There will always be new heights to attain. There will always be more innovative ways to do whatever you are doing, so you must make sure that you stay fresh, rightly informed, and motivated. Keep your content fresh if that's your thing. Keep your resources fresh. Keep your workouts fresh. Keep your lessons fresh. If you are good, become better. If you are better, become the best and if you are the best, strive to outdo your previous best selves. Remember, growth is the only stat relevant on the success road—growth per action, growth per word, etc.

2.) Let The "whys" Be Clear

The importance of motives can never be overemphasized. Communicate that *why* to yourself, your organization, your family, your pack, your tribe, your team, and whatever circles within which you have found a place. All must know what drives and motivates you to do the things that you do. When adversity comes, those "whys" are what will keep you from shaking or falling; and for them to do that, your motivation must be stronger than whatever forces of opposition may come your way. They will be your shield when you need protection and your sword when you need to attack.

When Buster Douglas knocked out perhaps the most feared boxer in the history of its sport, Mike Tyson, he had a "why." He told his mom he would be the world champion just days before the biggest fight of his life, only a short time before she passed away. He beat Mike Tyson in what is commonly thought of as one of the biggest upsets in the history of any professional sport. His "why" was greater than any punch Mike Tyson could throw at him that day.

I read a story of a 140-pound mom lifting a car to save a baby. She had a strong "why."

You can't have a sustainable plan without a "why" because the task at hand doesn't involve an emotional connection.

With relationships being the true power grid in your universe, remember the 90% rule. Ninety percent of all relationships, in any capacity, get terminated because of communication–either you're really bad at it, or you don't do it at all. The biggest deal-killer in business is lack of communication. So have a *why*, communicate that *why*, and let your *why* touch lives. A winner touches the lives of the people they associate themselves with.

3.) Create a balance between success and humanity.

Your humanity is not a barrier to your success. It is a catalyst for greatness. The intention of this book is not to make you a robot or a person to whom success is a drug that trumps every other thing in life. As you strive to become a winner, do not do away with your core values, beliefs, and morals. Nobody should ever have a reason to question your humanity. Let doing right always be more important to you than winning. Don't prioritize your quest for wealth or fame over your integrity. Don't be so hell-bent on being right, or you will miss opportunities to learn and improve. When you are constantly trying to prove that you are right, you are going to get stuck. The more humane you are, and the more you place a premium on giving back to your office community, your neighborhood community, your roster, and/or your circle, the more you will see success in a new light. At all times, you must have just the right amount of humility and humanity.

You must have just the right amount of humility and humanity.

4.) Be clear about your core values.

Be clear about them for yourself and others. Making your values clear to you and other people is nothing to feel guilty about. Clarity is a superpower. You must have boundaries. You should not be a self-righteous person who makes everyone else feel six inches tall, but there should be lines that you would never cross, and people should know not to cross with you. When you are upfront about your core values and clear about what you believe in, everyone's culture is better. The environment you operate in is more positive. Your family's better, your circle of friends is better, your roster is better, and people start seeking you out rather than having to recruit others to you. People want to be a part of what you bring to the table. People who hold the same values as you and are willing to work with you will easily know what you are about, and those who don't know to stay away. You can be authentic, and you can feel good about that. An additional perk is when you are clear on what is important to you, decision-making gets a little bit easier. You do not have to ponder too long on what you can or cannot put your hands into. The result is you tend to live feeling blessed, not stressed, leaving you with a positively infectious attitude.

5.) Serve.

You were put on this earth to serve. You were built to serve. Serving your best self, serving your community, serving your tribe. Before you become a servant leader, you must first follow. You must ride from the bottom before you get to the top. To be the best version of yourself, you must learn to submit and learn from those who have achieved what you expect to achieve. Even after you have risen to greater heights, you must still have that service mindset towards your clients, employees, teammates, and other people you come in contact with. Being a leader means serving those whom life has put you in charge of one way or the other.

This book, our courses, and our speaking engagements are all services to you and all those whose lives will be touched by the knowledge you will gain from here. Your service to humanity doesn't have to be on a very large scale. You may not be able to touch the whole world but make sure that you find a way to touch the lives of at least five to fifteen people you encounter every day. Studies show you will influence at least fifteen people today.

It takes no special ability to serve, and all great leaders do it. If you're not happy, you're not serving. Food, favorite candy, a favorite movie, sex, or watching the World Cup knockout round are all impacted by the same area of the brain. If you're not happy, take a look at if you're serving or not because those two are tied together and play a significant role in your attitude and the vibe you're sending to those around you each day. If you serve your circle, it'll be really hard for you not to be abundantly happy.

6) Embrace the Dust.

Sing in the face of adversity. Embrace that fertile dirt. There is good stuff in there. Don't let rough patches kill your spirit; dust yourself off and move on as they always say but don't rush into standing up. Make sure you also find whatever treasures are buried in that ground where you lay, as there is always something to take away from adversity when it comes. Before a seed germinates, it has first to die. This same logic applies to your life. Before you can grow into a fully rounded individual whose life will bless others, you have to implement the three Fs; FALL, FIND the treasure, and FORGE ahead. Take advantage of those failures and challenges, use them as a ladder to climb onto higher ground. When you fall in the dirt, recognize the flowers and fruits while plucking the weeds representing fear, doubt, and uncertainty. Never forget to weed the negatives and feed the positives. I've found that as I shift my thinking, I change my life!

Innercise

Innercising refers to exercising your mind. In life, we are constantly faced with battles. One can even argue that life itself is a battle. We wage both internal and external wars every day of our lives, from little things like choosing which foods we like to bigger decisions about a career or a country to move to. We are constantly contemplating what choices to make. Many times, we are conflicted on whether to relax our morals and values or hold on to them. Today can be the day you choose to get out of your own way and decide that never again will you choose to settle for anything that is short of your birthright to success. You, your family, your team, your workspace... you won't be staying where you are. There are plans for growth, promotion, and purpose ahead for you.

You may not be able to control all your circumstances, but you will always be in charge of your reaction to them.

I'd like you to imagine for a moment a long, large spectrum. On one side of the spectrum is circumstance, and on the other side are your feelings. While most will believe that it is the circumstances that lead you to your feelings, that simply is not true. It is your thoughts that connect those two dots. By confronting you and recognizing big feelings, you can disrupt thoughts and rectify bad decisions before they're even made. It is your thoughts that lead you to your feelings. What would be possible if the thoughts you, me, and we have were to be defeated? If you wish to have the *DNA of a Winner*, you must understand that life is not about what is and what is not fair. Instead of having the mindset of self-pity and victimhood, you must take charge of your emotions and forge on. Innercize your thoughts, and these trials can be the wind beneath your wings.

We cannot alter the past or handcraft everything in our future, but we can control the attitude we start each day. Imagine the possibilities if today, you decide to see yourself as a conqueror able to win any battle you enter, the possibilities if today, you visualize who you could become if you chose to attack any task thrown at you, or the possibilities if today, you decide to carry the approach of believing in yourself and having the courage to go outside your comfort zone? It's never too late to innercise those desires. This is the perfect time to stop settling and start igniting those flames that have been long dead in your mind. You might not feel completely ready to take the next step, but you have to put your fears aside and do it anyway because if you keep waiting for a time when all the stars will align, it may never come. The growth zone, that zone just outside the comfort zone that pushes you beyond your perceived limits, can be uncomfortable and at times can seem radical, but that is where all the magic happens. You're not going to feel ready to take that next step ninety percent of the time because what's uncomfortable isn't going to feel right, BUT it is imperative on the Success Road. The spark that will ignite the flames of positive results in your life is a positive attitude...shaped in the Growth Zone. A positive attitude is the fuel that will drive you to accomplish extraordinary results.

A new mindset + A new behavior = New Reality

Mean vs. Anxious

Our thoughts determine our destiny. Our destiny determines our legacy. Our legacy is what we leave in others and sustains long term. When someone says that a person's mean, are they really mean, or are they anxious? When reflecting on moments you'd like to have back and words that you'd like to have back, in those impulsive and knee jerk type scenarios, were you aiming to be labeled a mean human being, or were you piggybacking off anxious feelings that led you to regrettable actions? Be careful about labels. Before you label someone as arrogant or mean spirited, be sure to pause and reflect to make sure that it is what they really are. Many times, people project characteristics that differ from what they are at their core. They might be anxious or insecure but project a facade of arrogance because they believe it will stop people from taking them for granted.

For you to be a successful individual, you must be a good judge of character and must be able to see through the fronts that people put up. This will help you retain the people who would have helped you bring your dream to fruition. Be sure to form your own opinion without bias, weigh the good against the bad and decide based on which one surpasses the other.

Try to cultivate the habit of empathy. Before you judge a person, make sure you have tried your best to put yourself in their shoes. You can never fully know what is going on in another person's life, in that office, in that home, in that meeting, between those walls unless you were actually in those places with regularity. You do not know about the things that keep them up at night nor about the experiences they have had that make them exhibit those character traits that you find annoying. You're still getting to know our own self from day to day. How well can you actually know others if you aren't in those locations with regularity? This doesn't mean that there aren't people that are truly arrogant or mean spirited and make life hard for others, but I believe that most of the time, something is going on under the surface that you don't know about. Hence, you have to do your best to cut them some slack. You cannot have a passion for impacting lives and not be compassionate.

Domino Effect

You, me, and we didn't come into this world, roll out of bed one day and say, "You know what? I would really like to be mean. Being mean would be super cool. Let's do that." I don't see that being the case. Just as the foundation of a house will determine how well a building can fare, people's backgrounds can also shape lives. A person who grew up in a gang-infested inner-city environment will have life views, morals, and values that will contrast greatly with those of another person who grew up in a gated community with wealthy parents and never had to fight to survive. Once, I had a conversation with a lady who had lost her entire family to a car bomb in Iraq. She then had to be shipped to the United States of America, where she had never previously been and not even remotely similar to the home she grew up in. It is safe to say that her outlook on life would be different from someone born and brought up in the USA and still has their family around. Not everyone will have the same perspective, so you must always make room for others. Our perspectives aren't all the same, and it's those varying perspectives that help us form stronger opinions. Remember that diversity and variety are the spice of life. Our perspectives aren't all the same, and it's those varying perspectives that help us form stronger opinions. Remember that diversity and variety are the spice of life.

Generally speaking, people don't just turn mean for little to no reason. They likely still have good in them, and you'll have to decide for your group's betterment if the person is worth the risk to keep them around. On a personal level, make sure your words match your heart. Do they lead to miracles or misery?

Remember that 80% of us are unaware that we're unaware. When we act out of character or have regrettable behavior, there's something that's leading to this. If you're serious about making the relationship work, you'll default to empathy, perspective, and caring before assuming the worst.

Did you see three or four first?

The root of anxious actually means divided. When we really break it down, anxiousness really means division, isolation, separation from ourselves, separation from our teammates. We're trying to figure out why this person's doing what they're doing? They're anxious about something. Those breaths can be different for everybody. One route is to inhale positivity and excellence while exhaling that energy vampire that's trying to steal your thunder.

You also may find yourself beginning to feel the need to build a façade to hide your real emotions. You may already have. Maybe there are things in your life that make you feel anxious and worried. I want you to know that those feelings stem from a place of separation from your true self. If you ever start to fall into that trap, that pit of anxiousness, the key for you is to choose to, no matter what, roll out of bed with an attitude of gratitude. Let your first thoughts everyday stem from a place of gratitude. You cannot teach others to control their emotions and always be positive when you haven't mastered the art yourself.

We have to be encouragement professionals. Not just for ourselves, but for the people around us. We've got to make a conscious decision to inhale with intention and exhale with intention. Take a moment to breathe, drop everything sometimes, and just let yourself go; BREATHE. Inhale positivity and exhale excellence. When you inhale fear, let it course through your body for you to then exhale peace, gratitude, and calm. The other school of thought is to lean into struggles and inhale fear or that vampire trying to steal your energy while exhaling peace, gratitude, and a calm heart mentality.

Caregiver Mentality

The best leaders are caregivers. You will see this characteristic seemingly effortlessly shown by good teachers, coaches, and health workers who have a passion for their jobs. The best way to become the best at what you do is to consciously make sure that you add value to others' lives as you go about it. Create energy by adding value to others. People often attend conferences to learn new information from the speakers and connect with other bright minds also attending. These are the types of people who become great networkers. They put effort into looking for people whose lives they can be a blessing to and vice versa. They understand that you are always one conversation away from changing your life, so they invest in relationships that help them grow and become better versions of themselves.

You are always one conversation away from changing your life.

Invest in relationships that will allow you to be a better version of yourself. You're in the business of adding value.

Fear is a liar

Say no to any thought that will prevent you from trending up. You DESERVE to trend up. You deserve better. The negative thoughts that you have in your head are always a result of outside influence. They do not come from you. When you start to find the fruits of fear in your heart, be mindful of the following:

- Energy can neither be created nor destroyed, only transformed. Running from your fears will not get rid of them. You must inhale them and then exhale them in the form of productivity, growth, and positivity. Be aware the same holds true in how you project your energy to others. When you're excited, what will your growth/word stat line look like? If you're positive, it'll look really good. If you're negative, remember that while you're temporarily releasing that negative vibe, you're also giving it to somebody else, not getting rid of it.

- The negative thoughts you have in your head aren't even yours. They're not even coming from you, and we can't fix the inside issues with external solutions. There has never been a thought found inside anybody's head. Slumps? There's no such thing as a slump. A slump is just your perception of reality, a false paradigm made up, a figment of our imagination. It's not real.

- Stop listening to yourself and start talking to yourself. Those thoughts in your head are most of the time from outside influence, and your mouth will only speak what your mind is full of. You must renew your mind through your words, don't bring in those negative thoughts from the past. What happened ten seconds ago happened ten seconds ago. Fill your head with positive beliefs, commitment, persistence, and tough-minded optimism.

- Choose the attitude of welcoming those fears, anxieties, butterflies, and positive adrenaline that accompany big conversations, big games, and big moments. You didn't roll out of bed this morning to be mediocre, and you haven't lived to this point in your life hoping to not be in moments that matter. You deserve the best.

- Don't run from it. Inhale it and then spit it out in the form of productivity, growth, and positivity.

Choose the attitude of welcoming the fears, anxieties, butterflies, and positive adrenaline that accompany big conversations, big games, and big moments. You didn't roll out of bed this morning to be mediocre, and you haven't lived to this point in your life hoping to not be in moments that don't matter. You deserve the best.

The Edge

Nobody and no element have an edge on you without your permission. You must give your permission, whether actively or passively, before anything and/or anybody has an edge on you. An attitude to choose blessed over-stressed and tough-minded optimism over pity city negativity depends on what you give permission. Many people have knowingly and unknowingly given permission to fear and other negative emotions when things become too intense or because they felt it was convenient in that moment. We all know examples of high potential people with bright futures who stunt their growth and never achieve their high performer potential because they gave permission to things that eventually destroyed them.

The fact that you can feel fear means that you have the potential to feel other emotions, especially the positive kinds. You feel fear many times because you care about whether you fail or succeed, you care about whether your work is good enough, and a whole host of other cares. Care is a positive emotion, and your ability to feel it means that there is an engine of positive thinking inside you waiting to be started. There is always more than one side to every emotion you feel. Make sure to continually feed the positive sides because whatever part you give more food will develop better. Positivity is food for the soul- feed your soul with optimism. Feed it with belief in the right things and ultimately feed it with love as love is one of the greatest tools you can use to dispel fear.

You have soul ingredients in the tank already. You were born with them. Now let them grow and create space for your best self. Use your moral compass to drive you, and rather than getting hung up on the things you could lose, choose to get hung up on the things you could win this day. It is a great feeling knowing that you have the power to feel gratitude in any situation and understand you have the ability to choose whether you give permission to the circumstances or not.

You have soul ingredients in the tank already.

I have a son on the autism spectrum. I remember the car ride back home after he was diagnosed; it felt like I had been shot in the gut. I was heartbroken. I began to think of what his life would be like growing up in a world where people are judged by their ability to be like everyone else. I couldn't help but imagine what school would be like for him. I thought of people staring at him in grocery stores and at the park, trying to understand why he was different from anybody else, their faces leaving none of their thoughts to the imagination. These thoughts kept rolling through my mind, but less than fifteen minutes later, my wife and I decided to move forward and choose an attitude of gratitude for the little man. If we, his parents, were already envisioning such a hopeless future for him, what chance did he have? Not for a second did we ever believe we wouldn't give him the best life possible; autism is just such a difficult playbook to learn. Feeling sorry for him would only have truncated his destiny and kept him in a box. Instead, we started to plan, brainstorm, ask questions, and strategize ways to help create the rockstar he is destined to be and become a fulfilled man in the future. We turned the mindset of fear that we had at the beginning into one of optimism. My wife and I are lifelong educators. We knew what was coming in the years ahead in the realm of social health. We knew that there would be bullying, struggles to make friends and other uncertainties. In the end, our commitment to the best self-mentality, the success road, and choosing the right attitude as frequently as possible gave us all the juice we needed to help our son have an amazing life. He's the greatest kid, and we're so proud of him. None of that could have happened if we had stayed on that anxious train. You don't need to have a kid on the spectrum to jump on the positive train or choose a champion's attitude. All you need is fifteen minutes to decide that you want to live life as the conductor of your own positive train.

Weed out the negatives and feed the positives.

CHAPTER 2

The Double Win

What uniform are you wearing?

Being tenacious only requires you to be your best self. Give all you have, not more than you have. If you give your all, you give yourself every opportunity for possible success, and the Double Win as the iconic former Pacific Lutheran University Head Football Coach Frosty Westerling phrased it. *The double win is bringing out the best in oneself and others.* Dress yourself today with the double win uniform and mentality. While there are no guarantees for the outcome you're seeking, I can, with confidence, predict you will get the best shot at living the most fulfilling life possible for as long as you're wearing this uniform, the Double Win uniform. Trying to be something you're not, wearing a uniform that doesn't fit or is on backward, will result in disastrous outcomes. Stay in the Double Win lane, and you'll not only give value, but you'll receive value as a result.

You are a river, not a reservoir, the gifts and talents in you are not to be stored, they are for your good and the good of others, the more people fetch from you, the more you get, but when you are constantly full of all the things that have flown into you in the past, you will become stale and unusable.

We share this platform where we raise our leadership lids to become a better version of ourselves, create a better environment, create a better culture, lift up our communities and embrace struggle. If I could infuse one simple character trait into your life that has changed lives for everyday people, just like you and I, would it be something you're interested in? What we're talking about is the double win. If you have the DNA of a winner, if you have the DNA of a champion in life, if you wish to leave an impact on those you care for, this is something you must be intentional about. You must have the double win mentality for breakfast, lunch, dinner, and the snacks in between. You must be all about it. You can't put a price on people's lives, shaping community, or creating a culture of optimism. The fact that you have read this far into this book shows that you are at least in some ways emotionally invested in the double win mentality. You want to be the best version of you and want to be a champion for others.

Feel

The memories that dominate your mind are those that made you feel; whether good or bad, sad or happy, you remember them easily because when they happened, your mind registered the emotions that coursed through your body. The childhood memories that you have now are of those times when memorable, emotionally tactile feelings occurred. This same principle applies to all people; they might never remember your face or the gestures you make with your hands when you speak, but they will surely remember how you make them feel.

I can remember everything, from having to search for my retainer in a dumpster at lunch in elementary school to Brent Alvord's laugh as I lay at the bottom of the dog pile after winning a state championship in baseball as a senior in high school. I can remember the hurt and the ache I felt when a young lady told me that a texting driver had killed her mom as she cried on my chest. My wedding, my two sons' births, watching the highlight of my nephew hit a half-court basketball shot to win a game. As these pictures form in my mind, I relive these moments in small ways as the emotions flood my veins. You will not remember everything that your AP calculus teacher taught you or everything that you learned from your educational psychology professor. They gave you some good and valuable information, but what you will remember is how those teachers made you feel. You will remember those times they made you feel relevant, accomplished, and warm inside. They made you feel important. They made you feel like you mattered. You didn't feel like a number to those influential figures in your life. You weren't just a spot on a roster or a spot on the schedule. You were relevant, and they made you feel that way every day. Whether they were having a good day or a bad day, they were going to make sure they did everything they could to make your day great. You remember stuff like that. That is a classic case of the double win as I can guarantee you the mentor/coach/authority figure felt great reward as well. The double win is achievable for you because it takes no special ability to be kind.

In the beginning, it might take some effort because our default as human beings is to think first and second of ourselves before others. When you decide in your heart to cultivate a habit of kindness and put effort into being kind, it will get easier. What is your first thought when you see someone in distress? Do you sit and watch for entertainment? Do you go on your way like you didn't notice? Do you stand around and wait for somebody else to intervene? Do you stand around and shake your head in pity? Or do you step in and do all that is within your power to help? Your answer to this will give you an idea of where your kindness level is and where it needs to be.

The Best Self Travels

Your best self-travels fearlessly. It approaches the world with a mindset of readiness and is prepared for all the obstacles on the road to fulfillment. It is ready to go 24/7 at home, at work, on the field, and says to the world, "I'm ready to rock!" When you operate on that high frequency of being the best version of yourself, you will attract networking opportunities. People love to work with optimistic individuals who will help carry their dreams and establish them. Generally speaking, people love to hire those in the Best Self uniform as the best self-mentality shapes a winning culture. Best self gives companies their best shot at their best financial bottom line.

As you have decided to go into the business of impacting people's lives, do not limit yourself to only those you deign to be "normal" or "willing." Always remember that no two people are alike, and everybody negotiates and navigates through life differently. Acknowledge everyone's humanity and try your best to tailor your words and actions towards people in a way that will meet their unique needs. The way you relate with an outspoken and outgoing person may not be the same way you relate to another person who is introverted and isolates themselves from people. Make sure to test the waters before you dive in. You may not need to do too much. Just a sincere "how are you?" can go a long way in making a person feel better about themselves. Whenever you come in contact with anybody, no matter how short or long the period lasts, make sure they feel seen, heard, and relevant.

Why is it that we see people every day sitting by themselves or isolating themselves in a meet, and we can't muster up the effort to at least acknowledge their existence? I've never understood that. Now, maybe there are people like my son on the autism spectrum that enjoys being isolated from larger crowds and isn't a social butterfly. But by and large, most people don't want to be by themselves. They're not choosing to be by themselves. They're by themselves because maybe they don't have the courage to go up to you or go up to anybody. Maybe they're depressed. Maybe they've got something heavy going on at home. *Maybe*, you could create a double win, and you could be the person that goes over and says something to them. It might just be, "Hi." It could simply be a head nod, but just acknowledging them makes a humongous difference.

You can be a leader and not be THE leader.

W.I.N. What's Important Now. What's important is that you set your lens on the right things immediately. Be a difference-maker and a culture shaper with your actions today and create limitless Best Self opportunities not only for you but for those around you. You can do it. There are 365 days in a year. That's 365 opportunities to be a game-changer for somebody and shine a ray of warm light into the hearts of those that you cross paths with. I'm no statistician, but I believe that each day we have as many as fifteen opportunities to positively influence somebody. It doesn't matter who you are. Understand that to be a leader doesn't mean you have to be *the* leader. You do not have to wait until you are the leader of a worldwide multinational firm before you start to make an impact. START NOW, in that little church, that small community, that obscure group. Just plant the seed, water it, and watch it grow. You can be a leader in your community, in your workplace, on your team, in your neighborhood, anywhere! You can do this 365 days a year. That's pretty powerful. All you have to do is make sure that in your sphere of influence, no matter how big or small it is, you are making a difference.

Best Self on The Success Road

One of the most difficult mindsets to break is the road to success. The average person has a mindset where he/she has to reach the end of the road to experience any pay value. You do not have to get to the end before you begin to reap the benefits. As you go on your journey to fulfillment, there are rewards by the wayside that are there for you. Your self worth is not tied to your achievements or failures; it is not dependent on how well you dominate competitions or how many medals you win. Life is not a race to the finish line; it is a journey, and everybody has their own unique path to follow and an ETA that is also different from everyone else's. Put your focus on your BEST SELF and your own journey. Unnecessary comparison to outside noise will only do you harm. It is good to be result-oriented, but if your only focus is the result and not the process, you will become a robot.

By focusing on end results and not one's best self, we are losing the power of the mental game. As you go on your journey, pay attention to your evolution, see how certain experiences change your approach to life and alter the values you previously held dear. Don't be in a hurry to reach the end. Embrace the process and as you pass through life, let it pass through you too. Become self-aware on this journey and make mental notes on what you truly have a chance to be great at. I mention multiple times in this book that we all have Lebron talent, we all have elite thinker talent, but for various reasons, we leak those talents and don't ever get to see our true gifts.

Understand what you have a chance to be great at and punch the pedal in that direction. Many lack the self-awareness to understand what they truly have a chance to be great at and overextend themselves outside their greatness radius, creating a mediocre self. By focusing on becoming your BEST SELF, achievement and excellence can occur in the competitive arena and can repeat themselves far more often in the game of life. Winning is a byproduct of having an intense focus on things we can control. By having the right mindset with the SUCCESS ROAD, you have the opportunity to experience the DOUBLE WIN and never come out the other side the same.

The Unstoppables

To fully experience the Double Win, you must aggressively pursue the "unstoppables" below. They're the secret sauce in the DNA of a winner. Pursue them aggressively:

- Self-Awareness
- Value
- Morale
- Confidence
- Positive Culture
- Moral Courage
- Attitude

The double win adds value and awareness to lives. It enhances morale, confidence, a positive culture, and promotes moral courage. Think of the countless number of positive, natural highs you miss out on every day because you do not have the right attitude. To think like a winner, you must learn to think like a champion. Successful people aren't always in their position because they have more ability; In general, they're successful because they think a little bit differently than the average person. They may not necessarily work harder, but odds are. They most certainly work smarter. They understand where their efforts should be focused on. What does it mean to be a winner?

- Does winning on the scoreboard, your salary schedule, or high standardized test scores necessarily mean you're winning in your personal life? In your corporate world?

Once you learn winning in everyday life, it's all about traveling on the success road. It's a process, not a destination. Your daily pay value in life will increase dramatically. You will feel better about yourself and perform at higher levels because you focus energy and talent on things you have power over. The process needed to grow is kind of like chasing the horizon: You never really get there because it's dynamic, but the journey is incredible.

Unpack Your Thinking: Is success the end of the road?

Add value to just one person each day of the year and see the Double Win not only change your life but the lives of those in your circle of friends, your family, and your community. True leaders leave a legacy in the hearts and minds of those that follow their lead.

Unpack Your Thinking: We all know the importance of establishing enough capital to pay rent or maintain a business. What does it mean to build relational capital? How does it impact your social capital?

The number one reason adults leave a job/quit a position and the number one reason young adults quit a sport is they don't feel appreciated. Employees don't leave jobs–they leave management.

A toxic environment lacking gratitude is arguably the number one factor–this generally starts from the top down. No amount of financial compensation or bonuses will make a job worth sticking around for or a sport worthy of the hours needed to be exceptional. A great boss and/or coach is hard to find, difficult to leave, and impossible to forget.

Unpack Your Thinking: Does your style lend to creating an attitude of gratitude with others?

Throw Away that Savior Complex

Once, I was seated in front of my boss's desk in his office after being summoned. I was waiting for him to finish a conversation over the phone with another employee. When he was finally done, he made a statement that I will never forget. The moment he hung up the phone, he looked at me and said, "that guy forgot who he works for." This same person had been struggling for a long time to keep good employees around.

That statement might sound like a bunch of harmless words made in the heat of the moment, but I want you to know that that is not true. Those words show the type of mindset he has about leadership. It contains no iota of service or care. This is a picture of the classic Work *for* me vs. Work *with* me scenario. Do people work for you, or do you work with each other? When you refer to a colleague, do you introduce them as your assistant, or do you introduce them as a person you work with? One of those creates a toxic culture nobody wishes to be a part of, and the other creates a level ground, one where everybody is treated as humans. You do not need to announce yourself to be respected. People will respect you when they see the type of legacy you are leaving behind.

Most leaders who struggle know the right things to say but struggle with their actions. As a leader and trailblazer, you must be quick to show appreciation. It doesn't matter whether you could have done it yourself or if you are paying them a lot of money to do what they do. You should still use your words. One of the simplest yet powerful ways to show appreciation is simply saying, "thank you" and "please."

According to a John Templeton study of 2,000 Americans, we are *least likely* to feel or express gratitude at work, a common weak link in our best self-uniform. When we're listing what we're grateful for, our jobs come in dead last. It doesn't have to be like that. Sadly, the snowball effect of creating that missing link begins with our mental preparation leading up to the moment we open our door to the day. Wake up with an attitude of gratitude. Gratitude and calculated value-adding mentalities are where it's at.

When Doug Conant was CEO of Campbell Soup, he wrote approximately 30,000 thank you notes to employees. These intentional acts infused positive and caring energy into the company. This appreciation culture creates an environment of happy and sustainable relationships where everyone feels relevant and recognized. The work will flow easier this way, and there will be better results and more emotionally healthy individuals. You should never get to a point where you are too big for these words.

Below are ways to insert gratitude into your workspace or home life.

1) Incorporate a Gratitude Journal- Studies indicate more happiness and less depression in people who write down the things they're grateful for.

2) Authentic Thank You-Saying thank you can add instant value to your environment.

3) Gratitude Walks-Take 10–20-minute daily walks while reflecting on the things you're grateful for. If your first thought is that you don't have time, you must find a way to make time. Life indeed gets going fast, but we must *make* time for ourselves. If we were in a plane that lost cabin pressure, the first oxygen mask that gets put on must be your own. We can't best help others if we're not strong between the ears ourselves.

4) Believe it- it's not just about words or even actions because both of those things can be faked. Be sure that you are cultivating this culture because you truly believe that people deserved to be appreciated.

Traits of a Double Win believer

Moral Courage

A person with moral courage has sound thinking and good judgment. Moral courage is doing the right thing regardless of the circumstances. There is never a wrong time to do the right thing. What kind of human being are you if you're going to sit there and watch another human being treated like dirt for no reason? Sometimes we need to be the strength for others! We will run into situations where a person could be getting physically or emotionally abused, and we ask ourselves, "why wouldn't they leave that situation?" Unless you've been in those shoes, you won't understand it.

In another scenario, a person may be in a situation where they feel six inches tall due to a bully, and they don't have the strength to do anything about it. YOU can be their strength. We all have experienced situations where we needed somebody else to be our strength. Not every situation is the same type of scenario, so how you go about showing moral courage can vary. What you don't do is irrelevant because you have the DNA of a winner and a winner always does something.

Unpack Your Thinking: Would you rather be surrounded by people of integrity or loyalty?

Moral courage can also simply be putting your competitive juices in check and maintaining the focus on integrity and honesty. It isn't something you write in your business handbook. Integrity is how you and your team act when the lights are off. A group can get behind people with these human qualities and create a lot of momentum on the success road.

Unpack Your Thinking: Would you rather be right or do right?

Enlarging

Nothing that enters into your hand should leave you depleted or exactly as it came. As a leader, you have the ability to add value, enlarge and multiply. Let all that cross your path experience a positive change or enhancement. Team players love a leader who drives them to achieve greater success. Team players who add value to their teammates share a common characteristic–by adding value to others, they, in turn, add value to their own lives. There is no better feeling and what I've realized as I've gotten older; the more I give, the more I seem to abundantly get back in return.

"People aren't pursuing Ferraris; they're pursuing a feeling."
- Zenas Chin

The easiest way to win in the locker room or win in the office is to be an enlarging member of your community.

How do we become Enlargers?

1. Believe in others before they believe in you. Be quick to spot potential in people and waste no time in adding them to your team. Even before they see you for what you are, make sure you are already clear about their prospects. Let them see that you believe in them. When people know that you trust in their abilities, they will push themselves more and achieve greater success.

"I've never had anyone believe in me the way you do."

I received this text in the fall of 2019 from a client, and it made my day. If you're working together, you might as well put everything you've got into adding value to their lives.

2. Serve others before they serve you. You don't have to be great to serve, but you do have to serve to be great. Write that down, underline it, circle it, highlight it and say it out loud.

You don't have to be great to serve, but you do have to serve to be great.

I want to be that guy! Give them your best effort without any guarantee of return and be the first to do it. Do it not because you have to, but because it's in your DNA and you WANT to. Giving your best effort to be a fantastic human being and being proactive with these actions is the best way to go. It's also in the DNA of a winner. Serve the heart, not the talent and be consistent with these actions as only doing them a fraction of the time will give the perception that you're not authentic.

This is not the first-time service has been mentioned in this book, and that is because it is an integral part of leadership. Always lead by example. Show people how you want to be served by serving them first.

3. Add value to others before they add value to you. Be an inspiration, encourage those around you to be their best selves, take risks for them, empower them to build beyond their comfort zone but within their gift zone, point out their strengths and help them improve on their weaknesses. Even before they start doing anything physically for you, make sure that they can clearly see the value you add to their lives.

Positive leadership revolves around this concept.

Rise Up

I'd like to tell you a story about a guy, who we'll call Ray. Ray was a high school student of mine; I ran my class in a Socratic seminar-type format more often than not, which allowed students to engage regularly with their peers and me. Almost every day, we debated, and we discussed, and we argued and tried to stimulate one another's thought process. Ray was sharp as a tack, kind, a great worker, an exceptional human being, and first-class all the way. He was an OKG (Our Kind of Guy). Ray also had a speech impediment. I'm guessing throughout his life, he probably had people that didn't want to listen to him, laughed at him, tried to speak for him, or rushed him on while he spoke, thinking that it would help him.

But in my class, Ray was a leader. He would sit next to me every day and lead the discussions; Ray loved those classes. In the end, he wrote me one of the most heartfelt, uplifting, thankful letters I've ever received to this day. I believe that the difference between my class and all the previous interactions Ray had experienced was that I created a culture where he had a voice and allowed his best self to be revealed. The class was likely soothing for his soul.

As was the norm for all of my classes, I listened to him, made listening a non-negotiable premium character trait. Ray was able to share his thoughts and ideas, which were always brilliant and engaging. I'd imagine some of his thoughts in different environments were tougher to share before because people were not willing to hear him out. They focused more on how he spoke instead of what he was speaking about. Ray had always been a leader, even before he entered my class. He just needed a chance to be in an environment where he was seen as equal and relevant. A place where he was appreciated and respected and could function without the burden of other people's expectations on his shoulders.

Do you know a Ray? Is there an individual who needs a chance to be heard? Remember that when you continuously make room for people to truly be themselves, something happens to your heart, and you too become a better person even as they evolve. Ray taught everybody patience, acceptance, and appreciation that semester, just being his Best Self.

It takes a Village

We always hear the verbiage, "It takes a village." "It takes a village to raise children." "It takes a village to create a team, to create a workspace, projects," etc.–these things are all true. When you reflect on it, most of us were raised by a village our entire life: our biological parents, Godparents, grandparents, foster parents, doctors, nurses, babysitters, teachers, our youth sports coaches, our friend's parents, our neighbors, and even the world played a part in raising us into all that we are or are not today. All of these people have had a hand in shaping you, and along the way, they have dropped both temporary and long-lasting influences into your life.

My wife grew up with grandparents, great grandparents, aunts, and uncles at every function she ever had with school. They were a large part of her village. With my own mom, half of her entire family lived on the same hill in Virginia. Whether we realize it or not, they're all having a strong influence on us–their personalities, perspectives, how they relate to others, and how they treat others. All of those things naturally assimilate into our own lives. You may never personally trace what came from who, but those beliefs you hold so dearly and even your outlook on life were influenced by your entire environment.

How many of you have evolved with music as you've evolved with your circle of friends or co-workers? I'm guilty of this! Punk Rock, Rap, Country, the '60s, '80s, and today's pop have all been a part of my journey as I've bounced from what journey to the next. And as you move through life, you will find more people and things that will influence you, and you will drop some of the values you no longer resonate with and pick new ones because there is always room for development, and our Best Self is always evolving.

Embrace Vulnerability

Embrace it. It's a strength. Your vulnerability can be a strength, but only if you embrace it. Friction and resistance create bone growth physically, but they also create relational growth and personal development. Great leaders understand that they cannot shape a successful operation alone. The great ones recognize the strength that comes with togetherness, whether in sports, business, or friendships. They're intentional with relationships. While most run away from being exposed and showing vulnerability, I'd argue that exposure is a prerequisite to success in the right quantity.

Coaches should be exposing their players every day. A day, lesson, and or practice of never being exposed is arguably a wasted day of learning. The growth zone does not exist inside the comfort zone. Teachers are not teaching effectively if their students aren't in a constant state of safe vulnerability.

Exposure is a prerequisite to success.

Bringing everything to light; let your dealings be plain for all to see. Expose those areas that need to be strengthened, be real with yourself and others. Nobody is perfect. Even in life's crucibles, during the darkest trials of our lives, we can still find our sweet spot. And empower others to do the same.

Remarkable, Repeatable, Reliable

Speak these words out to yourself; ***Remarkable, Repeatable, Reliable***.

1. "I am remarkable. I am abnormally awesome. I leak positive energy!" You have what it takes.

2. "I am repeatable, worthy of emulation. I leave footprints in the sand for others to follow. I am a winner. I am a champion." You are the creator of your abundant life.

3. "I am reliable and consistent; I do my best, and my best is good enough." Energy grows where energy goes.

Today, go out and work like a champion. Play like a champion. Live like a champion because greatness awaits you. It's waiting. Be a champion. If not for you, do it for the people in your village.

CHAPTER 3

43,000 Thoughts Per Week

The Playbook to the Success Road

Ten-year-old Tucker Sullivan is a really cute kid. He's not a big guy, not the "get off the bus intimidator guy," but I tell you what, he packed a punch on this day! Late on a Saturday evening, I received a video text message from his dad, Ryan. I likely watched it 15 to 20 times, each time smiling ear to ear, giggling out of excitement with each replay. The 20th time was just as good as the first time. Tucker's a little ten-year-old baseball player. Before that afternoon's contest, it rained all morning, but the clouds later parted, the sun shined upon them, and the little ballers were able to fit a game in.

The game was tight, and families were on the edge of their seats as Tucker strolled up to the plate with the bases loaded in the bottom of the last inning. He comes up to bat, digs in, looks the pitcher in the eye, and hits a ball over the fence! His first career home run! Tucker hadn't even hit one in practice. He drills this ball over the wall, and that in itself is really exciting, but just watching the range of emotions from Tucker's mom and his teammates made it more special. I could hear his mom's excitement as she was recording the video when the ball was hit, and when the ball went over the fence, it was like her hair caught on fire. She was ecstatic!

On top of that, watching all of his teammates stream out of the dugout and huddle around home plate, waiting for this ten-year-old Tucker Sullivan to finish rounding the bases. Tucker coming down the third baseline, getting to the plate, jumping up and down, and landing on the plate, and then all of his teammates patting him on the helmet and just jumping as high as their little legs could go. The range of emotions was overwhelming. To see how excited the families, the mom, and the teammates were for the ten-year-old was heartwarming. Those are the kind of emotions that many in attendance will never forget and will talk about years later. The people in the stands felt it, people in the dugout felt it, and Tucker will remember that feeling for the rest of his life.

Bridging the gap between potential and performance is, more often than not, about understanding that success is not a destination but rather a process. Just weeks before Tucker hit his blast over the fence, he was in the dumps and running low on confidence. It's tough for a ten-year-old to fully grasp the concept of the success road, but we do have a shot at selling it if the culture of the roster is breeding it. Your office has a shot at being incredible if it chooses to hire culture shapers who are into the process. The road is full of adversity, milestones, happiness, surprises, and every emotion in the book. One must learn to embrace the struggles, become comfortable with the uncomfortable, and believe there is power to positivity and a chance to transform negativity.

Become comfortable with the uncomfortable

You must buy into the Success Road mentality if you are to achieve the best version of you and be a positive leader. Without a focus on the success road, it is virtually impossible to raise your leadership lid and be the kind of person people will want to follow. A lack of commitment to the success road creates an impulsive, knee-jerk reaction leader that frustrates everybody around them. You become selfish and overbearing. Choose the right attitude and bring positive leadership to your group. What we're talking about here is thinking like a winner. On average, we'll have over 43,000 different thoughts run through our brains in a week. We'll become what we think about.

Life gets spewed from your mouth, where miracles are bred. This is a choice. Say yes with me to the power of positivity.

Say these words:

- "I choose my words."
- "I speak only what I am and what I want to be."
- "Only uplifting thoughts run through my mind."
- "I choose to see only that which betters me."
- "My lips speak only life."

As you speak these words, make sure you believe them and concentrate your energy toward seeing them manifest in your life. *Feel* the words you're reading. Miracles can be bred today, victories can be made, and incredible journeys can begin with the choices, the thoughts, and the beliefs that stir within you.

Unpack Your Thinking: Can you think of a positive leader you've connected with? Selfish leader?

If I were to ask you, "Is success the end of the road?" what would be your answer? If you've got the DNA of a winner, you know that it isn't the end of the road. You believe it is the road. You will understand that success itself does not have an end. There is always more to be achieved and lessons to be learned. Success isn't a destination; success is a journey that you travel throughout your entire life. There is no period, only commas. You just have all these different things that happen along the way. And that's what I want to talk about.

When I was growing up as a young kid in high school, I was one of those guys who was everybody's friend but nobody's friend at the same time. I hung out with this obsessively clean guy who went on his LDS mission a month or two after graduation. I hung out with the guy that had a six-pack during break and everybody in between. I had a knack for having a bunch of different circles and just trying to see where I would fit in. I wasn't always a confident guy, but I knew right from wrong and tried to stay as close to the middle on the spectrum of good and evil as I could. If there is anything I regret about high school, it is that I attached my identity too much to my sport.

Where things started to kind of unravel for me a little bit was my sophomore year. I was described once as a "big kid who can run." I ran a 6.5-second sixty-yard dash once, which, if you know anything about athletics, you know was a significant achievement. An Atlanta Braves scout said to me in my junior year, "you can fly." But between my sophomore and junior year, I blew out my knee multiple times, sometimes more complex than others. As it turns out, my kneecap was too big for my knee socket and became an ongoing issue for decades. The first time my kneecap dislocated, it knocked me out for a baseball season and a football season.

Then going into my junior year, I broke one finger on my throwing hand. I didn't want to tell the coach about it because I was worried he wouldn't play me, so I played through a broken finger. Then my senior year, I ended up breaking my L-4, L-5, S-1 vertebrae in my lumbar back region. I really wanted to fulfill my dream of playing college baseball, but that dream began to flicker. As I mentioned, I tied my identity to athletics, to a fault. I sent out tons of letters, and quite a few colleges were sending stuff back early on, but as time wore on, fewer colleges came knocking. I'm not saying I was going to be the next Babe Ruth, or I was going to be on any Hall of Fame ballots, but I could definitely play somewhere. I decided to play one last summer and then move on to a pre-med major in college and a future physical therapist.

That summer was going to be my last hurrah. I caught a break two weeks before leaving for school being seen by a Houston Astros scout. He felt I was worthy of a recommendation to a couple of different schools, and I landed at one of them. That first year of college set the stage for the rest of my life for so many different reasons. The coach there was fantastic, the friends that I met there were fantastic. I was exposed to what confidence looks like and how I could embody it. I was exposed to independent thinking, accountability, and an extreme work ethic. All of these qualities can be difficult to uphold, but when you do, they give you your best shot at being your best self, and that was what I got to experience firsthand by being on the team. I wasn't a star recruit; I was a borderline guy to make the roster. I didn't play in our first 13 games in the spring. Yet, I led all freshmen in hitting, playing on a team with the nation's leading home run hitter. It set the stage for who I was going to be for the rest of my life. Hard work does not go unnoticed. Had I stayed in pity city and played the victim's card over and over like a lot of us want to do, it never would've happened.

Consequently, I never would've had the incredible opportunities I've had. If I didn't lean into struggle and ran from friction, I would be far from where I am now. If you're investing in you, friction isn't optional. Friction is necessary.

Sacrifice a Little, Live a Lot

Who you are today is not who you have to be tomorrow?

Bridging the gap between potential and performance is, more often than not, about assessing Wants vs. Needs. It's about understanding the Success Road and drawing yourself closer to the person you can become. You must always ascertain whether that step you are about to take is needed or if it is just something you want to do. To become your best self and accomplish your goals, you have to be disciplined. You must be able to say "NO" when it is necessary, even if it might make some family and friends displeased with you. The word "no" is a complete sentence.

"He who would accomplish little must sacrifice little; he who would achieve much must sacrifice much; he who would attain highly must sacrifice greatly."— James Allen

1. Give Up on The Unhealthy Lifestyle

This is a very important topic that many people take for granted. Many motivational speakers go on and on about achievement and reaching potential, but they neglect elements of health. Your mental, physical, and emotional health are all equally important. You can only be your best self and help impact others' lives when your health is stable. Listen to your body and pay attention to the signs. Prevention is always better than cure. Don't be so caught up in the grind that you forget to take care of yourself. Your health is the greatest form of wealth that you can have. Make sure you are never found wanting in the areas of:

1. **Quality Sleep**-how much varies with age groups

   Quality Sleep- no matter how busy you are. You should always find time to sleep. It does not necessarily have to be a long sleep. Several short naps will suffice. Just make sure you get as much rest as you can. Don't ignore breaks. Michael Jordan, Tom Brady, Lionel Messi, and Ichiro, all of the best to ever play their respective sports, took breaks. Lebron James takes breaks. The greatest CEOs in the world schedule break time. Seventy-five percent of our readers right now are probably going without adequate sleep. *Fortune* magazine estimates that the United States of America loses over $400 billion each year because they don't get enough sleep.

Be sure to get in as much rest as you can during breaks. Even traffic lights have a stoplight.

2. **Healthy Diet-**a balanced diet and when you eat is key.

   If you can afford it, do your best to eat well and healthy. Drink water throughout the day and be aware of your portions. Be careful about what goes into your body because that determines what response your body will give back to you.

3. **Physical Activity-**SMART Goals

   Have a vision in your mind of what you want to achieve with whatever task you set before yourself and your team. Let that vision keep you on the tracks of the Success Road.

S = *Shared*....set specific goals and share them with a coach, mentor, or teammate. It adds a little extra sense of urgency to meet those goals.

M = *Measurable*...many will argue that if you can't measure the goal, it's not much of a goal.

- What do you use for your scoreboard?
- How do you measure progress and envision goals?
- How do you evaluate people and set criteria?

- How are you evaluating people coming into your circle of friends, team, office, and family? What's on your scoreboard?

- Are soft skills a priority? If you want to have a great culture, you're going to look at character traits. Core values such as accountability, dependability, trust, and moral compass. Do they have integrity? Those kinds of character traits loom large in culture and tie directly to commitment.

If you tie your commitment to values, you're going to be a lot more prone to sticking to them. Conversely, if they're not tied to values, you really don't have any reason to hang on to them. In this scenario, there is an emotional disconnect.

A = *Attainable*...the best goals are both challenging and attainable. Your goals need to stretch you and be transformative, but they also need to be feasible. Both micro and macro goals are equally important. Set quarterly goals that are digestible and measurable every ninety days. Setting the ninety-day measurement for goals will give you room to monitor, judge your progress and adjust goals to fit your abilities and how far you intend to stretch yourself.

R = *Relevant*...the goals need to be realistic and relevant to you and your tribe specifically. Not everything pertains to you. The fact that it is good does not mean that you must subscribe to it.

T = Timely...always set goals with time frames attached to them. This will help you be more orderly and involved in the process. It will also give you a sense of urgency, which you will need to achieve the goal.

Those with the DNA of a winner set goals religiously and shape those goals around their core values. Those core values should blend in with the vision you have in your business and your personal life. Whether they are work goals or personal goals, schedule some time to unwind. Schedule "cheat days" for resting. Schedule "free days" to decompress. Schedule "fun" by design both in the workspace and personal time.

If you want to have a competitive advantage in life, in your business, in your relationships, with your team, you've got to have core values held loosely. Winners live a life where they roam freely within their own set of core values and, as a result, create more space within themselves.

2. Give Up The Short-term Mindset

"You only live once, but if you do it right, once is enough." — Mae West

Successful people set long-term goals, remain focused on the road, and realize that these decisions are merely the product of the short-term milestones they need to do every day. Such good habits shouldn't be something you're just doing; they should be something you're embodying and behaviors that are considered part of your DNA. Refrain from becoming the "New Year's Resolution Guy." The guy that sets lofty goals only to cast them aside 3-5 weeks later.

3. Give up on Playing Small

"You're playing small does not serve the world. There is nothing enlightened about shrinking so that other people will not feel insecure around you. We are all meant to shine, as children do. It is not just in some of us; it is in everyone, and as we let our light shine, we unconsciously give others permission to do the same. As we are liberated from our fear, our presence automatically liberates others."–Marianne Williamson

If you never take calculated risks on opportunities or pursue your dreams, you will never unleash your true potential. Consequently, the world will never benefit from what you could have achieved. So, listen to your ideas, voice them, resist the fear of failure, refuse to listen to the discouragement from outside influences, and never feel guilty for wanting the best version of you. When driving, if your car begins to fishtail/skid, do you turn your wheel away from the skid or turn your wheel into the skid? You turn into the skid. You don't move away from it; you lean into it. Similarly, with life, you must lean into the struggles and live with intention in tension. Don't run from the struggles. Embrace them. Breathe in your fears, breathe in your struggles and exhale greatness into the world. Exhale value and your best self into your day.

Shrinking yourself is not humility. Just like everyone else in the world, you have the right to take up space. Constantly shrinking yourself to make room for others does not make you a better person. It just makes you stagnant and unable to achieve your full potential. Make sure that there is a balance. There are times when you must stand aside for others to shine, and there are those times when you must seize the spotlight. Never feel guilty for wanting the best version of you. Ever.

4. Give up your excuses

"It's not about the cards you're dealt, but how you play the hand."
-Randy Pausch, The Last Lecture

Successful individuals know that they are responsible for their lives no matter their starting point, weaknesses, and past failures. Accept your mistakes and move on from there. Make peace with the fact that you will make more mistakes in the future. How you manage the opportunities of today determine your future opportunities. If you choose to focus on your burdens, how can you be trusted for future blessings? If you choose to waste your strengths and energies you already possess, how can you be trusted with life's invitation to climb higher mountains? Today is an audition for the opportunities being aligned for you over the next 12 months. Do you want more? Prove you will be faithful with what you already have in your tank. Get rid of the excuses. Use the adversity you've run into, no matter how big or small, to stimulate the growth waiting ahead. That doesn't start on January 1. It starts TODAY! Own your life; no one else will.

Today is an audition for the opportunities being aligned for you.

You have unrivaled, untapped ridiculousness, ready to be seized. Go seize that good!

Fundamentals of Playing One Milestone at a Time

There are choices to be made at every point in your life, so never forget to make the right choices because the choice you make today will make you tomorrow.

1. Play one milestone at a time, confident and focused on each moment as it is played.

2. Take responsibility for your thoughts and actions within your journey. Behavior is always controllable. Elect not to be a prisoner in your own mind and awaken the freedom within you.

Freedom begins with your beliefs. If you don't transform the beliefs behind the behaviors, the changes you wish to instill in you and/or your culture will not stick long term. Until you're emotionally invested, the desired behavior is only short term. The DNA of A Winner is about becoming, not arriving.

- The goal is not to score. The goal is to *become* a scorer.
- The goal is not to write a book. The goal is to *become* a writer.
- The goal is not to fly a plane. The goal is to *become* a pilot.

Freedom will create space within you for empathy, love-based thinking, and inside out leadership and behavior that sticks.

You want to be happier, but you can't because of X. Notice what excuses are barriers for you and release them. You create your excuses out of thin air. They are not real and are typically made by those that don't focus on the process. Let your mind be the most liberating place you know, where you can be your truest and unadulterated self.

3. Commit to habits first, goals second

One of the best ways to achieve a goal is to see it as something you wish to become, not just do, see it less as a chore and more as a habit you are trying to cultivate. When you focus on becoming and not achieving, it is easier for you to sustain long term success. You cannot set goals that do not align with your habits.

- Decide who you want to be?
- What kind of a person do you want to be when your name is called in a tight situation? When there are twenty seconds on the line? When the rubber meets the road? Build your habit to support that.
- Know why you do what you do.
- What character traits do you want to possess, and what you want to accomplish in the game?
- Setting goals without changing your habits will get you similar results.

Unpack Your Thinking: Is listening a character trait?

4. Make your daily actions consistent with your goals. You get what you repeat. As mentioned previously, most leaders know the right things to say, but in toxic environments, those in the lead struggle to have actions that match up with great leadership.

Unpack Your Thinking: Do your actions complement the culture of your program in your organization?

5. Focus on the process rather than the outcomes of your performance. Outcomes are results that include at least some uncontrollable variable. Being process-driven is the enemy of perfectionism. Perfectionism is the enemy of the "idea muscle."

Unpack Your Thinking: Am I staying focused on the process?

6. Progress is becoming superior to your previous best self. Is that something you strive for? Do you place a premium on trajectory over current results? Do you try to become better than you were last week? Do you look for a way to learn something every day? Openness and curiosity are generally present in most people we view as higher-level thinkers and players. They're open to hearing other ideas and perspectives, but they are careful to filter and examine those they wish to adopt.

Curious learning is a fluent concept. It is something valued enough to be listed on the referral form by the US Navy. Leonardo Da Vinci was an elite thinker. Da Vinci's desire to learn was the driving force behind his largest accomplishments.

Unpack Your Thinking: How do I think others assess my ability to work toward being superior to my previous best self?

7. If rejection or fear of failure is stunting your motivation, put a halt to that mindset. Rejection is a part of life, and you should not let the fear of it truncate your dreams. Rejection, failure, and adversity, in general, are not detours but are all part of the journey. Be grateful for these opportunities as they are our greatest teachers.

Commitment is 100-100, not 50-50. Don't stop just because you're rejected. Rejections of today can become innovations in the future. It's true that before we succeed, we will probably fail a few times, but we can't let our fear of failure subject us to a life of pessimism. Fears are like shadows. They're both dark, and they're both creepy, but neither can actually hurt us. They only have as much authority as we give them and only control us with our permission. Nobody has an edge on you in life without your permission. The only way to avoid mistakes in your life is to do nothing, which would be a massive crime.

Nobody has an edge on you in life without your permission.

5-Minute Rule

If fear is stunting you, you're not alone there! If you're not feeling it, we all have those days, and you may be dangerously close to normal! Whether it be lacking intrinsic motivation or fear, you can try the 5-minute rule below and finish on a great note. Nine times out of ten, you'll be golden!

- Set a timer for 5 minutes
- Start the task. Just simply say yes to starting.
- Give yourself permission to stop after five minutes. If you stop, be kind to yourself and call it a win for the day.
- Nine times out of ten, momentum will kick in once you start, and you'll ride that momentum.
- The key is to simply start.

Big Time Principles for Big Time Situations

Success is often determined by the ability to choose the right attitude and by mental/emotional preparation. This area of life needs to be addressed every bit as much as the mechanical and physical preparation. The following principles may help when preparing an individual and/or team for those special moments:

1. Don't get hung up on the possibility of losing. Get hung up on the possibility of winning. Yes, it is a risk that you are taking, and it might not go as you envisioned, but you cannot let the possibility of failure be the thought at the forefront of your mind. You are more likely to fail when your mindset is negative. Instead, focus on the possibility of actually pulling it off and coming out the other side with smiles on your face. Worry never achieves anything. It only leads to more worry. Expect to win and believe you will win. This belief is a stronger power. The more you think like a winner, the more it becomes a habit to expect success.

2. Don't get hung up on the illusion of the event. Get hung up on the competitive nature of what's next. Big crowds, big venues, lots of competition for the same position-the event can take a person out of the game. You have put in the work. You are ready! Stay positive, slow down, and let your heart lead. You're destined for greatness.

3. Pressure makes diamonds, but it burns too: The right amount of pressure from the right sources can lead you to achieve great things, but when the pressure becomes too much and begins to come from those who do not have your best interests at heart, it is time to reeval-

uate. Take risks when you feel a push in your heart to do so, not because someone else did or said you should. When counsel and advice come from people you know who share your visions and aspirations and want to see you succeed, it might be wise to heed their words.

4. Don't get hung up on the results. Get caught up in the process. The success road will have you trending up and will help fend off the emotional roller coaster that is inevitable if your optics are off. Ask yourself, "Who is the type of person that could get the outcome I want?" Align your beliefs with the behavior necessary, keep your lens on what is important, and you'll see the process translate to happiness.

5. Don't get hung up on doubts, questions, and fears. Get hung up on knowing you are prepared to be comfortable in the uncomfortable. Only you can choose to slay comfortable and reach for your abnormally awesome. Choose to slay! You've practiced. You are ready. Robert Schuller once said, "the greatest churches have yet to be made." It is true. The best is yet to come. Stray away from the risk-averse society surrounding you and play life, ready to win the risk plays and create your own plot. You're destined for greatness.

6. Don't get hung up on the pressure of the moment. Get hung up on gladly taking the risk. This is why you compete. Take in the pressures you can handle and no more. It's not life or death. Go for it! Embrace it! You want to be in moments that matter. You don't grow up thinking, "I sure hope I can be in games that don't matter" or "if I'm lucky, I can have the opportunity to compete for a crummy job!" There is no real pressure on it. Pressure is finding a way to pay for rent at the end of the month when you have no money to pay.

7. Be an OG. Optimistic Genius. Open your eyes to all the positive possibilities, see the world through a lens of optimism. The ways to do that are:

- Get hung up on visualizing positives.
- Catch others doing good.
- See yourself achieving.
- Relish the opportunity to live out your positive dreams. There is power in being positive.

There is a competitive advantage to being a glass half full thinker. Now, can you be a glass half empty thinker and still make money? Absolutely, but it's an unhealthy lifestyle, not only for you but those whose lives you are meant to touch. You're unaware that you're unaware of the impact you're having on others if you're a glass half empty thinker. Fear holds a lot of people accountable. It also holds a lot of people captive.

8. Trust yourself, and believe in your abilities. Be confident enough to take your own side, know the types of things you can and cannot put

your hands into. What lies ahead of you has nothing to do with winning the genetic lottery, whether it be a big game, a big interview, or a tough conversation. Understand you don't have to be the best team or the best person for the job. *You only need to be the best that day.* Fifteen seconds of courage can create a conversation or a positive experience like never before. Fifteen minutes is enough for you to leave your mark.

Failure can only happen with your permission.

Keep a steady diet of positive thoughts. Trusting yourself is a competitive advantage.

Unpack Your Thinking: Why are you fighting so hard for your own weaknesses and lack of self-control?

9. Sing in the mud, dance in the rain. Be persistent. Work hard even when the circumstances are not in your favor, anticipate needing to sing and dance in the face of adversity. Success is a marathon, not a sprint. Never give up. Perseverate with positivity and understand that your why is greater than your knockdowns in life. Be a positive warrior!

10. Embrace the side roads. In your journey through life, apart from the distractions and the obstacles, there will also be perceived detours. There will be times when you will have to turn back and take another road. There will also be instances where you might need to pause and take a break. All these are normal and should be expected. Two roads can lead to the same destination. We need our plan Bs to ultimately find our best plan A. You've had to create a new typical your entire

life, most recently with COVID, but truth be told, you've been an evolving new typical since the moment you took your first steps. What's wrong with different typical anyway?

My favorite people on the planet are people that aren't typical at all. They're amazing! Being a good person does not tie in with typical. It does not depend on status in life, religion, race, skin color, political view, or the culture you were brought up in. Just because they're different doesn't mean they don't have amazing in their arsenal. You're going to create a new typical fifty plus times in your life. That in no way means that we have failed or our journey has been cut short. All it is is a bend in the road that will still lead to our preordained paths. You must evolve with the times and seasons, be ready to evolve and adapt and make the best of any situation that might come your way. Just as you have evolved over time, the person you were when you were ten years old is no longer the same person you are now, the same way the person you are now will be different from ten years to come. All life's experiences change and shape us in one way or another. Embrace the detours and take advantage of them

11. The Success Road isn't static. It is a living, breathing, rhythmic way of life that is always shifting in real-time. It's dynamic. So, it's always evolving as the world evolves. We were never set-in-stone, to begin with. We're not made to be a stick in the mud. You are built for change. Just as a programmer can program a computer to perform specific tasks by learning its code, you can program your life in the same way. You can enhance the way you live, shape your own culture, and code your life!

Take four seconds right now to raise your right hand as high as you can…………………

Now raise it higher……………………… Why didn't you raise it that high the first time?

Every story of success entails long hard hours of work. There is no getting around this. Most programs and companies have core values, but more often than not, they revolve around what is convenient for the moment rather than alignment with what serves as a true North for the program. The foundation of everything revolves around your core values and gives you and/or your team its best shot at redemption when that time arrives.

- Danny Shannon, The Gratitude Maker out of Australia, is a great redemption success story. One that has him escaping death 15 times, falling out of a three-story building chasing his next high, and one that ultimately has him clean, being a recovering addict and operating his own worldwide company. Danny didn't have his first memorable belly laugh until he was beyond 40 years of age. Today, he has one of the best laughs on the planet and spreads loved-based thinking to the world.

Redemption is fed by your core value machine. Repeat that. *My redemption is fed by the core value machine.* That is strong. Stay true to your values, and you can be unstoppable. There's nothing in your way. Now, this isn't to say that because you have dreams and goals and you're committed to your values and all that jazz that it's just naturally going to happen. But I can tell you this. It's going to give you your best shot. It's going to give you your best shot to win this day. It's going to give you your best shot to be 1% better.

Take the shackles off your wrist. Lift those weights trying to bear down on you. Lift them, chuck them, and embrace the freedom. Understand that greatness hidden behind the curtain of darkness is waiting for you. Gandhi didn't take a knee. MLK didn't take a knee. Walt Disney didn't take a knee. British author JK Rowling didn't take a knee. Why should you have to take a knee? Why should you have to bow down to these pressures? Why should you have to bow down to struggles? We all have struggles. The encouraging detail about those previously mentioned people is they were no different than you and me at one time. They were the same ordinary, typical, starting from the bedrock type of people we are. So why not you?

This is not to push the narrative that all those who never achieve potential were too weak or unserious because the truth remains that life will rattle you to your core. Life will punk you. My life is a small example of how disheartening the world can be. I have been budget cut, let go, passed over, underappreciated, limited physically, and the like. The devil wants you to quit and throw in the towel, but you've come too far to quit. You've come too far not to be at least 1% better. You deserve to become the best version of yourself. You can get up after being knocked down because it's part of your DNA, and the strength to persevere is embedded in your spirit. It's embedded in your mentality. It is part of the reasons why your life can be a positive influence on others. You are a different kind of beast. Say these words aloud to yourself:

- "I am positively different."
- "I have greatness in me."
- "I can finish this race."
- "I have the strength to take the next step."
- "I refuse to take in negativity."
- "I exude positive energy."

You're the captain of your own ship. You've got unstoppable fire within you. Find learning moments every day so you can get better. Understand the road to success IS the road, and real commitment to the road leads to redemption.

Your Best Self is waiting, and it does not discriminate!

Unpack Your Thinking: Can commitment be tied to the ability to be attentive and/or focused?

CHAPTER 4

Culture Isn't One thing-
It's Everything

Sing in the Mud

Culture is a dynamic, constantly evolving process built by design. Uplifting workplace environments, positively energetic classrooms, mutually beneficial friendships, and united teams all stem from conscious efforts. Words can topple down or establish empires; if you are not satisfied with what you see, you can change it with affirmations that align with what you want to see. You have the power to choose what you think about and how you go about pinpointing positives.

The coffee bean.

If given the opportunity, would you choose to be the ice cube, the jellybean, or the coffee bean? The cube looks the part on the surface, but the moment things heat up, it melts and disperses the vibe to all those around it, ready or not. The jellybean, too, looks well put together and passes the eyeball test. It's firm on the outside and looks the part, but deep down, it's soft and can be squashed with little pressure. The coffee bean, on the other hand, does not mislead us. It presents itself on the outside the same way it is on the inside. It provides an entirely different environment with its presence, and that's the kind of OG you want to be. You aren't trying to have something; you're trying to become something. You want to be the optimistic genius.

When things get hot, the coffee bean rises to the occasion and adapts. The coffee bean impacts its culture positively, making everything around it better. That is the type of person you want to be, the one that has the right tools for every occasion. Fearlessness is not the absence of fear; fearlessness is reacting bravely in the face of fear. Coffee seeds are ground and put in hot water to form coffee.

In the same way, you can transform with the heat into your best and most useful self. You can transform culture positively with what you choose to share and the path you carve out both verbally and nonverbally. You can be a positive group that creates a positive culture NOW. It's a choice. Be the coffee bean.

Cultural Check-Up

- What do you like best about the present culture of practice with your team/group? What do you think should be done to achieve that improvement?
- What is the root cause of your culture?
- Are you an active participant?
- Are you looking to recruit extraordinary people to your circle??
- Are you continuing to edit, enhance, and transform your own beliefs?

University of Washington football, Duke men's basketball, Oklahoma softball, New England Patriots football, and virtually every great program in every sport has a culture that creates a winning mindset. Starbucks and Chik-fil-A have made customer service and culture a massive priority within their organizations. There are plenty of relevant organizations out there, but each program's way of conducting business and thinking determines how sustainable that establishment will be.

Unpack Your Thinking: How do you build influence and maintain culture?

One of the many things I admire about the sports sector is how well they abide by set precepts. The codes of conduct are followed to the letter, and whoever deviates from them will most certainly face the consequences. Most successful sports programs have written down values they live and operate by. These values can be described as their "way." The Patriots way, the Boise State way, the Yankee way, etc.

Many will come up with unique descriptors such as the Lady Vols Tennessee with their Daily Dozen or USA Basketballs Gold Standard. In each case, their "way" is the foundation of their program and their core value. Like a beaded necklace, the team is strongest when together and all in tune with the way.

The values are instilled within every individual from top to bottom the moment they begin their journey/training. Full buy-in from the members of the organization maximizes the team's chances of becoming the best version of themselves. Being their best self will ultimately include winning big games and closing big deals, but winning will be the byproduct of being on the positive train, treating each other well, and adding value to the lives around them.

What is the "way" of you and your team?

- How well does your *Way* attract elite performers to become a part of it?
- What is your *Way* of competing?
- In what ways does your *Way* help your organization? Or do they hinder it?
- How would you describe the current *Way* of your organization?
- Does your *Way* align with your core values?

The Power of Yes

We have established that words have power, both negative and positive, but the word *Yes*, in particular, is extremely powerful. It can be the difference between life and death for a person too far down the donor list in critical condition. It can be the first word among a million on your way to success. *Yes*, is the reason why you are in this world today, running the race with everybody else. *Yes*, can also be negative. It can mean the beginning of your downfall, an end to positivity in your life. Be mindful of your selectively aggressive actions and say *Yes* to concepts that have you trending up.

When clinicians and therapists advise patients to turn negative thoughts and fears into constructive affirmations, more often than not, the quality of communication begins to improve, and the patient regains self-control and trust. But there is a problem; our positive words and thoughts are barely recognized by the brain and need constant feedback. They're not a threat to our security, so the brain doesn't need to react to positive thoughts and words as we'd like.

To overcome this neural bias for negativity, we must consciously generate as many positive thoughts as possible. For each negative thought that enters your mind, you'll need to generate at least three positive messages to counter it. I'd recommend reading the book *Talent Code* by Daniel Coyle to learn the science behind our ingrained habits.

Even if those positive words and optimistic feelings feel unfounded or useless at that particular moment, don't stop thinking and saying them. Release them into the atmosphere, and they will come back to you when you need them. Life is a constant struggle to stay positive, so if you don't need them today, they will be useful tomorrow. Joy will not find you if you don't actively search for and embody it. To be joyous means you brought the joy to the table by design. It doesn't find you; you find it. Full-time positive thinking will help you create a healthier attitude to life both inside and outside of where you work/train. It can be part of a behavior changing, life-altering outlook. It will add value to your life and those around you. There's something to the power of being positive. Positive words and thoughts propel the brain's motivational centers into action, and they help us build resilience when we are faced with life's problems. If you want to develop lifelong satisfaction, you should:

- Regularly engage in positive thinking about yourself.
- Share your happiest events with others.
- Savor every positive experience in your life.

Consistent positive vibrations are the catalyst for success. You do it. You enjoy it. You do it again, and you celebrate it again. Suddenly, you begin to see consistent results. Ironically, *goals can be the largest inhibitors of happiness.* The issue with a goal first mentality is that you're never actually celebrating your positive experiences. You're continually putting happiness off until the next event and viewing it as something for your future best self to enjoy. It's a vicious cycle. Savor, Share and Engage in the celebrations found on the journey. Focus on the habits and the systems that lead to the goal(s) you desire, and your journey will carry less stress accompanied by an abundance of happiness.

If you want to be celebrated by other people, celebrate yourself.

Additionally, having a solid social network of friends and teammates is important. You're only as good as the people you surround yourself with in life. Surround yourself with positive warriors, and you will start taking on positive warrior habits.

These thoughts can become. Many people create a learned behavior from an early set of experiences. With negative experiences, the patterns get stuck within the subconscious mind and can literally shape who you are and how you respond to your environment.

Try your best to stay away from negative dialogue because the more you engage in it, the more difficult it becomes to stop. A negative frame of mind, more often than not, creates a negative snowball effect with both yourself and the team. Avoid the mistake of speaking in anger. Be conscious of the fact that words, once said, can never be taken back. Negative words, spoken with anger, do massive damage. They paralyze productivity. They send alarm messages through the brain, interfering with the decision-making centers in the frontal lobe, increasing a person's propensity to act irrationally. Take a day out of the week, and consciously speak only positive words. As time goes on, increase the duration, and when you have done it for a substantial amount of time, sit down and evaluate the difference in your life and how you feel.

Your thoughts and ability to say "yes" to a great attitude can alter lives.

Unpack Your Thinking: What kind of impact can an inattentive person have on the people they work with? Friends? Family?

THE NON-NEGOTIABLE TRAITS OF A GREAT CULTURE

The Teammates Who Play Together, Stay Together

Here is a clear character profile of the ideal team player. Being a team player is another piece of the puzzle when trying to be a positive leader with a winning mindset. While individual talents contribute to the team's success, character, positive body language, and having healthy relationships with the people you go to work with play a large role in building the necessary rapport and cohesion with teammates; it's also necessary to be a quality human being. It's important to understand that you should not do these things because you're hoping somebody notices or sees your good deed(s). You should do them because it's a part of your DNA and who you are or who you want to be. When others start to notice and believe in you, they will do that on their own accord, and your culture will take off.

1. Collaborative

Collaborative: Working together ultimately cascades to winning together. When it comes to achieving expectations as a team, collaboration is the keyword. Cooperation is simply working happily together, but collaborating means working more aggressively together. All the parties involved aggressively put all their resources into the work to make sure that it is a success. You may need to change in one of the following five key areas to be a collaborative team player:

1) Perception- Is the perception you have of yourself accurate with the view others have of you? Do you look at yourself with the eyes of the world, or do you look through the lens of greatness? Are you unaware that you're unaware? Do you smile?

Unpack Your Thinking: It takes roughly 13 muscles to smile. Conversely, it takes 60+ muscles to frown.

Do you check up from the neck up each morning before conquering the day? Whether it be squeezing in 10-15 minutes of meditation or simply spending time thinking about what is next or what you're grateful for, start each day strengthening your mental hygiene.

2) Attitude- You have a choice between the blessed attitude or the stressed attitude. It is impossible to feel both at the same time. An attitude of gratitude and an attitude of servant leadership is paramount to your success. Servant leadership is an honorable route to travel as it is adding value to others.

3) Focus- Laser beam focus on the right details.

4) Belief- Belief is influential, as much as knowledge and sometimes more. These three steps will help you achieve everyday belief.

1) Spiritually- This can be faith-based, or it can be whatever higher power you feel comfortable with.

2) Mentally- YOU! YOU! YOU! Believe in yourself. Believe in your ability to achieve great things and *become the blueprint*. Create for yourself the reality you want to believe in, see a home where there is empty land, light where there is dark-

ness, see hope when all things seem to be going south. The six inches between your ears is the biggest difference between good and great.

3) Physically- Ninety percent of what a person gets out of their workout comes from how they take care of their bodies at home. This includes sufficient amounts of sleep. Lebron James spends approximately $1.5 million on his body each year.

4) Listen- The largest contributor to terminated relationships and communications is the listen to reply guy syndrome. People don't listen to understand; they listen to reply. What you don't want to be is the *listen to reply guy*. We all know that guy, that person that cannot wait to start talking. You're in the middle of your sentence, and they're constantly cutting you off, or right when you're done. It's as if they've already got an answer ready to rock. They haven't even been listening to you. They're putting a comma in the conversation when there should be a period. You don't want to be that guy. You want to be the person that makes them feel that you are all in, that their feelings matter to you.

In a world where people struggle to listen, constantly cutting each other off and assaulting each other's thinking, it is important to internally promise not only yourself but to those in front of you that you will be an engaged listener. The biggest mistake most people make while listening is when they try to express their ideas and feelings and make those the priority. In reality, what many people want is to be listened to, respected, and understood. If you want to meet another person's needs and make them feel dramatically better than they did pre-conversation, then you need to listen to them. You need to ask good questions, genuinely wanting to learn from others and about others. To develop solid relationships, you must be quick to listen and slow to communicate. You don't do this because you have to. You do it because it's part of your DNA.

2. Communicative

A great organization has many voices with a single heart. Communicative team players do not segregate themselves from others; they're into servant leadership; they make it easy for others to communicate with them. They give attention to potentially difficult relationships. If you play your cards right, you communicate by design, and you make it a priority to be very good at it.

Rule of 90-The Rule of Ninety postulates that ninety percent of all relationship failures are because of poor communication. Either the person doesn't communicate at all, or he/she is just really bad at it. To improve communication, one is expected to:

- Be transparent, be authentic, but do it tactfully. There should never be a question about your integrity. It must be plain for all to see.

People always make statements like, "I don't play games; I just tell it as it is." But this is not always the best approach. Sometimes tactfulness can be the difference between life and death. Before you speak, chew the words in your mouth and see how they taste to you. I used to have that mentality when I was young. I always said, "I like it when people just shoot me straight, so that's how I'll operate." Research indicates that a large percentage of the world's population believe in this ideology. This is why many interactions in our world today are shallow, never deep, because people fail to understand that they must treat other people the way they would love to be treated in an ideal world. I like it when people shoot me straight. I want people to be real because I always want to know where I stand. But there's such a thing as timeliness. Saying the right thing at the right time, knowing when not to speak and how to speak when it is time to speak.

Once, I had some issues with a groundskeeper in the school where I worked. He wasn't maintaining things the way he should have been, and I was really frustrated with him. One day I let them have it. I just went after him and spoke my mind; I was very upset that he didn't care as much as I did. The next day I got called into the principal's office, and my superior said, "Brad, what's up with this? What happened?" I explained to him that there was a certain way I wanted people to work with me, "I just want people to be straight up with me," I told him, "I shoot from the hip, and I don't play games, I just tell it like it is," My principal replied, "Brad, we all play the game. It's just a matter of how well you are playing." *We all play the game. It's just a matter of how well you are playing the game.* How well are you playing the game? You're in it. You woke up this morning in it. You will go to bed tonight, still in it. You're in the game. It's just a matter of how well you are playing the game. Are you tactful? Networking is one letter away from not working. No one wants to work with that guy.

It's a great lesson I learned, and I'm so thankful for the opportunity to be in front of a leader that cared enough to communicate it in a way that I hung on to it.

- Be decisive, but at the same time, don't make a rash decision.

- Be inclusive. Include others by design.

- Be the boss you always wanted. A recent survey indicated that the most rewarding feeling coming out of an eighteen-week seminar was inclusion. It was meeting new people who otherwise never would have crossed paths with or been given a chance to meet. It was the process of bringing people together that gave them the best feeling, more rewarding than anything they'd experienced in that arena. You wouldn't be reading this right now if you didn't have warmth in you and a desire to bring people together. When people see that you're genuinely interested in their lives and their wellbeing, in addition to others around them, your relationship becomes an emotional investment. People will want to work with you because they know you genuinely care.

- Be empathetic and caring. Take the feelings of others into consideration. Being empathetic focuses on awareness of how other people feel, an important and vital trait to being a great friend, co-worker, and/or teammate. However, caring goes one step further and focuses on a process of action that will help others.

Ex.- Empathy......."I understand how you're feeling"
Caring.........."I want to help."

- Trust. Money may be the currency of transactions, but trust is the currency of interactions. Great interactions lead to the only currency that never goes bankrupt; that is relationships. Additionally, trust creates space within us for creativity and allows us to win the risk plays within our work, sport, and/or relationships.

Author **Seth Godin** on having good ideas:

"People who have trouble coming up with good ideas, if they're telling you the truth, will tell you they don't have very many bad ideas. But people who have plenty of good ideas, if they're telling the truth, will say they have worse ideas. So, the goal isn't to get good ideas; the goal is to get bad ideas. Because once you get enough bad ideas, then some good ones have to show up."

5) Learn everybody's name, asap. It's tough to connect if you don't know the names of those you work with. Learning their names shows an emotional investment and kindness and gives the feel of relevance to the people you cross paths with. This attitude prevents resentment and bitterness from building up in their hearts and slowly eating through the team. It also gives them a sense of responsibility and presence; they will not feel like shadows in the background that can get away with anything because they don't matter. There is power to having positive interactions–no matter how big or small.

Unpack Your Thinking: What kind of energy am I transferring to others?

2. Perception = Reality

People's perception of you is their reality. Right or wrong, it doesn't matter. You could be extremely hard working, but if their initial feel on you is that you are lazy, you will be lazy in their eyes and the eyes of those close to them and so on. If your public image is skewed, life will be harder for you. It doesn't matter what you think. It matters how you're perceived. You can't close deals, you can't create bonds, and you can't be a go-to person if you're perceived in the wrong way. If you want to be in a top-notch environment with a positive, high octane, and productive vibe, the perception of you needs to be high energy and passionate.

3. Enthusiastic

Your heart is the source of energy for the team. Your passion is fuel for those that walk into the same room as you every day. Enthusiasm is contagious and feeds you and your team's intrinsic desire to be exceptional. Your tribe needs to know that you are fully dedicated to the work, and they also need to see it in your actions. The oil flows from the head to the rest of the body. In the same way, your enthusiasm will flow to the rest of your team.

Culture doesn't take days off, and it doesn't have to graduate. Shape the culture of your space with the powerful connecting tool of enthusiasm and passion. Take responsibility for your enthusiasm, don't always act how you feel, and believe in what you're doing.

To improve enthusiasm, one must:

1) Embody a sense of urgency: if something is important to you, you do whatever it takes to achieve it quickly. Ironically, many of us are slowed down because we've been trained to fear our own needs. Like a weed choking out a garden, the lack of urgency to be our own best advocate can be fatal for our desired outcomes. However, what's exciting is we can learn to work and communicate when we are fearful in the same way we have learned to grind through our days when we are tired.

2) Be willing to do more: Always be willing to go the extra mile for what you believe in. To do more, many times, you have to be more. Meaning, high performers generally think and work at a different level than the average worker. Additionally, you must align your energy to your values.

Energy Audit

- *What elements give you that ready for the day, roll out of bed, ready to rock energy?*
- *What elements give you neutral energy?*
- *What are your energy vampire energies?*

3) Strive for excellence: Never settle for less than is attainable. You have the DNA of a winner and a champion, so resist settling for what

is just "okay" or "manageable." Your work should always be exceptional and measured up to the best self-effort.

Unpack Your Thinking: What do you do when other teammates don't appear as committed as you are?

Never forget in your pursuit for excellence that the secret of creating a rich investment for you is to create a rich investment in others. A love-based approach, operating from the inside out. It has been proven repeatedly that a loved based business approach and a love-based culture create an environment that gives you and those in your circle their best shot at being their best self. Stay positive and forward-minded with those that don't appear to be as committed as you but be careful to know when to let go so that the work is not negatively affected.

4. Intentional

Make every action count. Being intentional means working with a strong sense of purpose.

- Why are you settling for a cheap and easy life?
- Why aren't your eyes wide open?
- Why isn't your heart beating out of your chest with excitement?
- Why didn't you expect today to be totally unforgettable?
- Why is your passion not bursting out of you and touching every soul you come in contact with?

Is it possible that life and unexpected, tough-to-anticipate experiences collectively, gradually, and slowly made it all just "okay?" Is it possible that you've settled on okay? Don't allow life and all its surprises and struggles make you gradually begin to settle for just "okay." Don't give up on your dreams because you haven't yet seen the light at the end of the tunnel. You will gain nothing from stopping now, only regret and wasted time. Is it possible your team has settled for just good enough? The moment that "okay" mentality begins to be normalized, it will not be long before the mindset of failure dominates. It's time to take back what is yours! It's time to take back that full life you were put on this earth to live. It's time for you, me, and we to take back that abundant life that has been dormant in you, waiting to be seized. Circumstances don't change who you are at the core.

You want a culture you can operate in, and you want to have fun doing it. Why would you want to roll out of bed and not want to be a part of something fun and productive? Having meaningful conversations with everybody you're involved with as many times as possible each week, even if only for brief moments-those are relationship building and culture building moves. Those are moves that create an awesome culture and pave the way for a really good Success Road. Productive people never get confused and haphazard. Most moments in our life become special only when we decide internally to make them special. *The average day is average only because we make it average*. Make the most of your opportunities!

5. Prepared

Success loves preparation. If a big-time opportunity presented itself today, would you and/or your group be ready? It's better to be ready and not have an opportunity than to have an opportunity and not be ready. To succeed, you must be ready before the opportunity arrives. Preparation can mean the difference between winning and losing. To improve preparedness, you must:

1) Be a process-oriented thinker. This will encourage big picture thinking.

2) Research and prep for your moments. Failing to prepare is preparing to fail.

3) Learn from your mistakes, embrace struggle. Be willing to embrace your scars.

"The secret of success in life is for a man to be ready for his opportunity when it comes."–Benjamin Disraeli

6. Relational

The true power grid in life is in relationships. From the moment you step in to the moment you step out, fostering healthy and mutually benefiting relationships should be THE priority. Adding value to others should be the first strategic move you make as a leader. If you get along, others will go along.

As previously mentioned, a large portion of your success will be determined by the relationships you've built with your coaches, teammates, clients, coworkers, etc. Teams want people who are relational and people who will be compatible with the existing chemistry. Good mentors can teach you the content of their operation; what they need in a hire is a person who is great with relationships and great at connecting. Connecting happens not when people understand but rather when people feel understood. Being a fantastic listener is a valuable character trait and a bridge to greater relationships.

It should be noted, the people who work with you tend to buy into your ideas more when they feel connected. The right connections trump the significance of more connections. To better relate with others, you must:

1. Focus on others instead of yourself- *Focus on the Double Win*

2. Ask the right questions- *understand the power of asking good questions, listening with intent and having good follow up questions is an art form that works magic.*

3. Share common experiences- *Vulnerability is a strength. Storytelling is a strength. There is no greater bond between strangers than that of shared experiences.*

4. Pinpoint positives to make others feel good about the right things- *In the end, all team members need to be thinking about the right things at the right time in a positive manner.*

One common mistake leaders often make is wanting to hire "yes guys" and trying to surround themselves with people like them and never challenge them. A great leader understands that it is important to have other perspectives apart from their own. This helps both to strengthen the ideas they already have or give them a new and better way to do the same thing. Additionally, as a positive leader, you need to have the ability to work with individuals that are not alike and bring them together.

7. Self-improving

Throw away the mindset of "this is the way I am." As a person in the business of changing lives, you cannot afford to think like this. You must constantly reinvent and improve yourself. You cannot be talking to others about achieving potential while you remain stagnated in your thinking. Lead the way for others to follow. Value self-improvement above self-promotion.

A great culture has a wide range of personalities and different types of workers, but by and large, a great culture has a large percentage of self-starters. .

A great culture has a large percentage of self-starters.

If the superior has to coach effort, the organization isn't going to have long term success, and it's going to have cultural issues from within. Getting harassed to give more effort creates tension, and having to be the one harassing is zero fun.

Value self-improvement above self-promotion.

- Your goal for today is to be better than you were yesterday. It is not to earn a title or a position or to have bragging rights. If

> this world truly is about relationships (and it is), you will only be separating yourself from others in a negative fashion if your motives aren't honorable. You never want to get in a position where you're having people play "for" you or work "for" you. You should always have the humility and courage to allow others to work with you. Your goal is to help lead others to the top–not get to the top by stepping on their heads.

Unpack Your Thinking: How well am I budgeting my leadership skills?

8. Evolving

The world is constantly evolving, so you should too. Teams often deal with changing conditions and also create change themselves to suit the times and seasons. Good team players roll with the punches; they adapt to ever-changing situations. They don't complain because something new is being tried or some new direction is being set. Any coach, any teacher, any leader who has ever designed a plan understand that plans do not always go exactly as designed. The best can adapt, can anticipate change with a solution mindset, do a great job with whatever circumstances settle in front of them. The road to success is not a straight line. It is full of curves, has bumps in it, has its ups and downs, but is ultimately necessary to improve your previous best self.

To roll with the punches effectively and be able to take a reflective step back, try one of these:

1. Keep a journal: Spend 10-15 minutes several times per week writing about whatever is on your mind. This is an effective form of reflection, and it can be an antidote for confusion! This is also a powerful exercise for dealing with internal issues and unresolved problems. This process allows you to express yourself in a way that works for you.

2. Schedule "Reflective Time." Pencil in one day each week where you can reflect on the current week and also plan ahead. If you want something different from what life has currently handed to you, you're going to have to do things differently. If you want to live the abnormally awesome life you deserve, you have permission to live abnormally awesome. You have to critically look into your life and change the parts that do not align with that mindset. Individuals who recognize they possess the DNA of a winner think differently. If you want what the general population has, then live the lifestyle of the general population. *You are seeking a lifestyle*, not a position, and not a skill set. You weren't put into this world to live in someone else's movie. Command yourself to do what you know has to be done. It won't be smooth sailing at first, but you have all it takes to succeed within you. Your think tank is ready, and your future best self is waiting.

3. Snipers and Babies. Mindset Coach Zach Brandon compares meditation to that of babies and snipers. With both the babies and the snipers, breathing patterns are part of how they concentrate. Babies are always taking big belly breaths. Snipers

actually time their shooting between heartbeats. Pencil in five to fifteen minutes/day for meditation. An awesome perk to mediating comes through breathing patterns. Learning how to breathe brings a competitive edge to your life. Most people realize they're not breathing from the right areas. One of the most common mistakes unknowingly made in more intense situations and nerve-wracking situations is allowing breathing patterns to dramatically increase and shift in a way that clouds decision making. Meditation is useful to:

- Create space in your mind and turn your muscles off so that you can relax and only the right emotions course through your body. This can be relaxing and calming, easing stress levels.
- Brainstorm. Many use this time to create their best ideas, manage their days, and do it in a non-threatening, relaxed, controlled environment. It may be the only time all day some of us can make a decision without the outside noise.

One misconception about meditation is that you have to be 100% focused while conducting it. *Studies show that 47% of people have wondering minds while meditating- almost half*! There is tons of space there for you to wonder while creating freedom and love from within! Just do your best to focus on your breathing and try to close the gap with your wandering mind.

Meditation doesn't have to be about your specific sport or your specific place of work. It could be about a problem that's eating away at you, schoolwork you're struggling with, or visualizing positive vibes/moments.

If you don't create space for five to fifteen minutes to meditate each day, you're missing out on a lot. The best organizations on the planet incorporate meditation into their routine, hiring mental coaches and hiring professionals. If the best of the best are carving out time, why shouldn't you? The best part is awakening your freedom and creating space inside you for kindness, for value, for the hustle and all it entails-it's all free!

9. Functions as an active participant:

Organizations that have been able to maintain a great culture and positive energy for a long time have done so because of the presence of active participants. They're fully engaged in the work of the team and do not sit passively on the sidelines. Those types of people in whose hands a dream can never die; they are constantly looking for ways to contribute to the organization's growth and development. Sometimes such people do not come ready-made. They are created as a result of the inclusion and acknowledgment culture. When everybody in the organization feels a sense of ownership and responsibility for all that goes on in the business, they become active participants.

These active participants also understand the difference between trying hard and being positively competitive. Any person can get pulled off the street and try hard, but positive competition means the person plays life with max effort, concentrates on the right things at the right time, and he/she can make adjustments based on feedback.

For example, if you're running in a competition to be safe, you're not competing. You're just running. Taking risks is an important part of your journey on the success road. If you are always playing it safe, you might be unable to achieve complete fulfillment. As you engage in healthy competition, don't forget that your best is always good enough.

10. Committed

There are no halfhearted champions. Commitment is usually discovered amid adversity, and committed people don't surrender easily. It takes no special gifts or abilities. Instead, it is the result of choice. A choice to resist the "kind of" syndrome. You "kind of" want to do it. Well, if you "kind of" want it, then you're going to "kind of" get the results you're looking for. A person that's committed doesn't ever do "kind of." It's not part of their vocabulary. They're all in. You see this in relationships, you see this as an athlete, and you see this in the office. I don't see too many great ones "kind of" going after it. Open up your eyes today and see what you were created for. Open your eyes to seal the leaks where the "kind of" syndrome has seeped into your life. You weren't brought into this world to be "kind of" good. You and every member of your circle is a walking, talking miracle that deserves better than that. Commit to it.

Commitment lasts when it's based on values. If it's something you believe in, it's easier to keep. If it's something you've invested in, it's tougher for you to fold.

To improve the level of commitment, one must:

1) Tie commitments to values.

- Honesty- be clear and straight.
- Authenticity- be yourself.
- Integrity- your actions match your words even when nobody's looking.
- Love- wish them well.

"When you train your employees to be risk averse, then you're preparing your whole company to be reward challenged."–Morgan Spurlock

11. Don't Be Afraid to Be Different

Be different. Be abnormal. Follow your conscience, not the crowd. Following the herd is a sure way to mediocrity, and you didn't wake up today to be mediocre. You want to establish a culture of independence and a tribe of outside the box thinkers who can come together with the group's best ideas as a whole.

Ask yourself:

- "What would I do if I wasn't afraid?"
- What would be possible in my life if things which have held me back were defeated?
- What if the fear was conquered?

The good ones all think a little bit differently. The exceptional groups don't wish to blend in. Be selectively aggressive with your actions, and resist the urge to be in someone else's movie. Create your own slot.

Unpack Your Thinking: What is something you believe in that others think you're bonkers for believing?

All of us get caught up in limiting ourselves by setting boundaries about who we think we are and what we believe we can achieve. Coaches, management, parents, friends, and teammates have an opportunity to enhance a person's self-image and self-confidence by encouraging each player to believe he can achieve as much as is obtainable. People, who don't feel good about themselves, rarely accomplish great goals. Helping others feel good about themselves is a part of being a great teammate. Find the good, praise it, and build on it.

Unpack Your Thinking: What one improvement could you make right now that would improve your mental toughness by 25 percent in the area of "Don't Be Afraid to Be Different?"

CHAPTER 5

The Best Self Does Not Discriminate

Accelerate People Potential

Is it reasonable to grow one percent every day?

In their entirety, these things might seem too difficult and unattainable. That is why throughout this journey, I have advocated for taking things one step at a time. Over time, many of these concepts have become cliché. All our lives, we have heard people say things like "expand your horizon," "achieve your full potential." Like some sort of religious mantra, making it easily ignored and even despised. But this does not negate the fact that these things are achievable in real-time. We all know people who made these things a reality in their lives. We know those names we look up to and mention when we give examples of greatness. What is stopping your name from being on that list, even if it's just in your small community?

A great goal is one that is both challenging and attainable. 365 x 1.01%= 37% increase in happiness. This is a bold challenge, but the payoff is massive and allows us to fail forward if we don't reach it. This mentality gives us our best shot at being our best self. The best self has no boundaries, doesn't care what color your skin is, couldn't care less what part of the world you're from and it travels. Every one of us can be 1% better today. Regardless of where your starting point is, whether you're a seven-figure salary guy or happier than a gopher in loose dirt, we all have something better inside of us. We can be 1% better today. If your best self-environment were optimized, what would your life look like? What strengths and passions would you be leaning into?

Best Self Mentality

This concept does not advocate infallibility. Being your best self does not mean that you never have days when life gets to you. It doesn't mean that you will never make mistakes or that you will always be cheerful. Being your best self doesn't mean that you will be perfect. Your best self is that state of complete awareness, one where you are not deluded about your shortcomings. It is a state that seeks to constantly improve itself, one that is sincere and willing to learn. The best self-mentality is the key to unlocking many positive doors that have been shut in your life. It is the ladder you climb to success and inner peace. It is why you will be a trailblazer and an example to those who will come after. To be your best self, you must:

- ▪ Be truthful to yourself and others around you.
- Be ready to accept when you are wrong.
- Take responsibility for your actions and their consequences.
- Love yourself enough to spread that love to others.

- Accept the things you cannot change and strive to change those that you can.
- Believe in yourself and your penchant for success.
- Know that you are strong and able to take on the world.
- See yourself through the mirror of greatness.
- Take your dreams seriously that all who come in contact with you will catch the fire.
- Know that you might fail sometimes, but you are not a failure.
- Be kind.
- Be positive.
- Buy into the *DNA of a Winner!*

There is nothing righteous about being superior to someone else. Progress is becoming superior to your previous best self. Is this a goal of yours? Do you try to become better than you were last week, last month, last year? Do you strive for a noticeable difference every day? Are you striving for a point in your life where you no longer have to improve? You can't expect to be a great, selfless leader who is respected if you don't have the right mentality for it.

What we were told when we were seven years old and became numb to as we became older really was the truth. Do your best. To utilize the DNA of a winner, you need to focus on the controllable.

Two things that you have absolute control over are your effort and your attitude. These are areas you not only can control but can dominate. Many credible applicants and/or participants fall short not because they couldn't do it but because they tensed up, got tight, and tried to be something they're not. When you're tight, you play slow, and you don't always think with the same clarity as when your breathing patterns are normal, and your body is loose. If you give into nervousness, it is impossible to be your best self in big moments. There isn't a situation where you need to be more than you are; all that you are will suffice. If all that you are isn't enough at the end of the day, then it is likely that that feat wasn't really in the cards for you to accomplish.

Give Up the Fixed Mindset

"The future belongs to those who learn more skills and combine them in creative ways."–Robert Greene, Mastery

People with a fixed mindset think their intelligence or talents are pre-determined traits that cannot be changed. They do not understand that talent without hard work is dead. This is what we refer to as a behavior blind spot. There are blind spots in cars that prevent us from seeing what is going on in certain areas around us. Successful people are aware of such blind spots and do their best to limit their negative effects. They invest an immense amount of time daily to develop a growth mindset, acquire new knowledge, learn new skills, and change their perception to benefit their lives. Growth minded individuals believe they can always lift the lid of their leadership and expand their horizons.

More blind spots that you might be experiencing:

- Not delegating (Great leaders delegate).

- Tolerating "good enough."
- Being socially unaware and insensitive of your behavior on others.
- Blaming others for circumstances/victimitis.
- Treating commitments casually.
- Withholding emotional commitment.
- • Blind to your own mistakes and faults.

Unpack Your Thinking: Is good enough, good enough?

Unpack Your Thinking: What you track determines your lens. Are you trying to catch others doing good, or are you negative-nelly tracking? Choose carefully.

Unpack Your Thinking: Is your first impulse to take ownership or to pin blame?

Typically, people who are consistent excuse-makers/finger-pointers aren't confident and can be a bit insecure. They get caught up in what others think about them and lose sight of what they can control. As a result, despite these types of people actually having good hearts more often than not, they come across as selfish. The good news is they feel, which means they care. They care, which means you can help shape their mindsets. So, it is possible for you to help change their mindset and/or change yours!

The guy who thinks his stuff doesn't stink *doesn't belong in your thought radius.* When you have the DNA of a winner, you understand there isn't a strong correlation between best self-performance and areas such as age, race, gender, nationality, income, etc. Success is more tied to best practices of being your best self than it is in the previously mentioned areas.

We don't have to be the best. We just have to be our best.

Unpack Your Thinking: Is ASAP commitment or confusion?

I would argue that the phrase "as soon as possible" does not resonate with winners because, for us, generally speaking, ASAP is more code for I'll do it when it's convenient for me. ASAP doesn't really provide any specifics. It's open-ended, and there's really no accountability to it. Ironically, what ends up happening with many ASAP individuals is that they dump their workload on other people when they eventually do not deliver, consequently adding stress to others' lives. This move alone obviously doesn't mean the individual is a crummy human being. Still, it does end up being an energy vampire move and stressful to those who are accountable, caring, and emotionally invested. We want to reduce stress, not only in our own lives but in the people we care about and the people we work with.

Unpack Your Thinking: Would you rather always be 10 minutes late or 20 minutes early?

On the Other Side of Fear is Fulfillment

Don't be focused on the enormity of your opponent. Don't focus on the size of the task sitting in front of you. Get hung up on knowing neither *can claim an edge without your permission.* Your opponent may be the big corporate rival or the undefeated monster no one wants to battle with. Give these thoughts no grounds. Walk through life knowing that you can and will win. Believe. When you refuse to give in to fear, you will find fulfillment.

Unpack Your Thinking: If you could have one gigantic billboard anywhere with anything on it, what would it say?

Whiners vs. Winners

Life is always happening for us, not to us. Instead of dwelling on your propensity to make mistakes, dwell on your ability to persistently overcome adversity. Feed on your ability to handle the adversity life throws at you and shape yourself to experience abundant life. Use the boxer mentality; when you get knocked down, you have ten seconds to get up. Do whatever it takes to recover quickly. This is what separates the winners from the losers. There are whiners, and there are winners. Don't waste time whining.

1) Get into the habit of learning. Seek opportunities to be your best self. *Invest in you!* It'll be the best investment you'll ever make.

2) Reevaluate your role on the team. What do you have a chance to be great at?

- One of the differences between those that are good and those that are great is that the great ones understand what they have a chance to be great at. There are plenty of "pretty good" ones out there that could be great, but they spread themselves too thin trying to be great at too many things, thus eliminating the chances of achieving their best self.

3) Think outside the box. *Be comfortable with the uncomfortable.*

- Learning to speak to an audience, getting on a bike for the first time, or learning how to walk again after an accident. These are all initially extremely uncomfortable activities, but with time, as you get closer to your goal and the picture of the outcome in your mind begins to take shape, you persevere and keep the faith until the end. Nothing in life comes easy. Even the things you think are easy still require some level of commitment and discipline.

Unpack Your Thinking: 21 Day No Complaint Challenge. Can you go 21 days without complaining?

CHAPTER 6

Happiness is an Inside Job

The magnet for health and wealth

Is your mind full, or are you mindful? Are you self-aware?

Are you consciously moving through life, or are you sleepwalking? Do you see yourself as a real person deserving of all good things and whose actions have real consequences? Do you judge yourself the way you judge others? What occupies your mind when you are not actively thinking?

WHO ARE YOU?

Many will travel a path and get to a destination that did not include them. Never at any point did they discover who they were in the pursuit of a job, title, diploma, or achievement. You're the CEO of a large corporation, you've reached a management level position, you're the starting quarterback on the football team, that's great, but who are you? Who you are and what you do are not the same thing.

These questions are important for everyone who wishes to trend up in life. Most people who think they are "woke," aware, or whatever word they choose to call it, are actually just moving through life with their eyes and minds closed. Are you one of them?

Eighty-five percent of the people out there think that they're self-aware, yet 80% of those individuals are not.

AMRAP

As Many Reps as Possible

Reps don't only matter when you are trying to get that summer body at the gym. Trying to form habits and absorb cultures requires you to be persistent. Are you squeezing in as many reps as possible? This is not about slinging iron around in the weight room or cramming a bunch of stuff into your day carelessly or without thought. I'm talking about meaningful reps, as many kindness reps as possible, as many diversity reps as possible, as many positive words reps as possible, as many gender equity reps as possible, as many reps where you're adding value, not only to your own life but those around you.

Are you squeezing in as many of those as you can? The one thing we can't recycle in life is wasted time. What will you do with the light of today? In life, moderate effort is only for those who want moderate success. If you want to be highly successful, then your effort has to match your expectations.

There's a big difference between high potential and high performance. People with high potential have a tall ceiling. It's clear as day for everyone to see. They can choose whether or not to use it. High performers may not have the privileges or advantages of the former, but what they lack in talent, they make for in hard work, discipline, and dedication. We want to be a high performer, and we want high performers around us. One of the biggest mistakes those in hiring positions make is assuming a high potential candidate is high performer material. Not everybody is management material, captain material, or head coach material.

You want leaders who will teach fun by design, embed empathy into your operations by design, shape influence by design, and build culture by design-with as many reps as possible every day they walk in the door. You want to establish a culture where people want to come back and where take-home value is abundantly clear on a regular basis.

The people who win are the people who show up and give value. The added value is what lures people back. It is the catalyst to squeezing in all those meaningful reps, to becoming 1% better every day.

The people who win are the people who show up and give value.

If we ask around your little or large sphere of influence, what would people say about you? Do people have testimonies that tell of your kindness? Or those that bring to light your selfishness? As you answer these questions, be truthful to yourself. You are the only one who knows the truth, and no one is lurking around to judge you.

Take it a step at a time, one percent better every day for the next 365 days. If you can get 1% better every day, for 365, that's going to be a 37% increase in your happiness! A 37% percent increase in happiness if you can just get 1% better at winning this day and staying on the positive train. If you're getting 1% better, this shows up in the way people perceive you. This shows up in the type of people that you allow in your circle. It shows up in your culture. It shows up in your "way," it builds your community, and it attracts winners. As you develop and begin to embody your true purpose, you will be unable to hide the changes and progress that will begin to happen in your life.

I know that for me personally, when I had major reconstructive back surgery on three different levels, my L-4, L-5, and S-1 vertebrae, I had to be really intentional about how I received therapy and how I learned to walk again. I remember going on walks with a stroller, and I had to plan in advance how far I was going to go because I still had to come back, and that took some extra effort. If I was walking alone, there was always a scary thought in my mind that I would be unable to get back home. With back surgeries, you have to be extremely patient and not rush the recovery, so walking back in a lot of pain would've been a bad idea.

The purpose of this story is to teach you a lesson on respecting your limits and working with them in mind to achieve the best results. There is nothing wrong with starting with small steps as long as you do not go on at the same pace for an extended period of time. As the CEO of Mind Valley, Vishen Lakhiani challenged people to dedicate twenty minutes of their day to personal growth. I challenge you to do it for twenty-one days. This would be a fantastic habit to help shape your new AMRAP mentality and goal setting.

21-Day Personal Growth Challenge

If you're getting better and seeing results, that's fun, and if it's fun, is it really work? Ideas to aid you in this challenge include listening to your favorite positive podcast, reading a book, meditation or writing in your journal. The great Viliami Tuivai once said, "You cannot add time to your life, but you can add life to the time you're given." The most popular class at Yale, one of the best academic institutions in the world, is how to live a happier life. The best investment you'll make today is the investment in you.

Kindness Calendar

Create a kindness calendar. Simply write a kindness goal and or task for each day of the month. Do something spontaneously kind for another person and/or set of people each day of the month. It might be for a friend, family, or even better, for a complete stranger. Record it in your calendar and review it when the set time is up. I promise you will be awed at the changes you would see in your life all around. This kind of culture creates happiness.

Examples:

- Perform a small helpful task for a friend or a family member. You'd write that small task into the calendar. It doesn't have to be a large task. Something similar will carry massive weight for them and will fuel your tank as well.

- Simply give a compliment to as many people as possible and be authentic about it. Simply write "Authentic Tuesday" on the calendar.

- You could write three thank you notes on every Thursday of the month and call it Thankful Thursday.

- Be creative with it and tailor it to meet your needs.

The end goal is to touch lives and strike chords, make people feel good about themselves, be intentional about engagement, lead and ultimately live a standard of excellence, and install happiness by design. Life's not always about working harder. Life can be about working smarter too. Many people budget their vacation time more than they budget their everyday lives. Create that Kindness calendar and get intentional!

Relationships Are the True Power Grid in Life

Relationships are the true power grid in life, and they are a currency that will never become obsolete. The connections and relationships you establish today will be instrumental in shaping the rest of your life. Networking is crucial and not just for pyramid schemes and financial gain. The word network is only one letter change away from "not work." If you build your network, you shape your life.

I can't think of a job I've ever earned where I didn't know somebody in the selection process or have some sort of networking inside the process. This does not negate the fact that I was still the best guy for the job but having established relationships in advance really helped seal the deal. This comes from understanding perception equals reality. How people perceive you is their reality, right or wrong. Let empathy be infused into your networking process.

- Is empathy a part of your pairing down system?
- Is it a priority in your think tank?
- Is empathy part of the process when you're trying to figure out who's in my circle, who's not my circle, who I'm hiring, who I'm not hiring, etc.? How do you evaluate that? Is there juice to that?

If you're an inside out thinker, empathy has to be valued. Understanding how others feel is a pillar to success. It's a staple to customer service. It's a staple to a good warm climate, and it's a stepping stone to being a great listener. On the flip side, language also shapes your life. What's your language like? It shapes your culture, and it creates your way. Seventy-eight percent of workers quit for preventable reasons.

Remember, listening is a character trait, and you want to be a high character person.

Seventy-eight percent of workers quit for preventable reasons.

This does not apply to offices and company settings only. It also applies to those who never finish or renew their gym membership, those that start a course and never complete it, and the likes. This applies to all spheres of life. Seventy-eight percent of workers quit for preventable reasons. Money is not all that matters. People want to feel safe in the organizations that they are a part of. They want to feel needed, relevant, and appreciated. They need a healthy work environment to flourish, and many times, this is not always available. It is possible for the general work environment to be peaceful but have one or two toxic people whose energy contaminates the atmosphere and makes it unbearable for others.

The responsible guy wants to take accountability for everything and ownership for his/her actions, but sometimes we step into a situation that needs a lot of damage control. While it's not always you, I do, however, have great respect for the first person who always chooses to look in the mirror before rushing to judgment.

So, what is your ultimate qualification for success? Is it love? The intriguing advantage to love is that it's got unlimited space inside it. UNLIMITED SPACE. What coach and/or CEO wouldn't love a roster full of people with unlimited room for growth? Interviews and tryouts are really about projection. Players and potential employees always assume that they need to be their best that day, and you indeed want to put your best foot forward that day, but scouts and most people in management will tell you that they're also placing a premium on projection. What does this person's ceiling look like? Is he or she tapped out, or is there room for us to grow together? This concept has ties to empathy, which ties directly to success. Success leads to progress, and progress leads to new doors of opportunities.

Every opportunity has three possible doors through which they can enter into success. The point of entry perspective varies from individual to individual.

1) Main entry- this is the door through which most people enter, e.g., high school, college, firm, etc. In this line, you've got all of your friends and family guiding and rooting for you. You are sure of at least the barest minimum, and there are always people to fall back on. You have the cushion of comfortable surroundings, and you're full of fresh recently passed on knowledge. It's the standard point of entry. The line is long, and you may not get in through the exact door that you desire. The facility is always almost at full capacity, having space for only a few more people. In the context of this conversation, a person trying to go in this door is assimilating with what the majority is doing and going to get what the majority else is getting.

2) VIP entry- This is an entry where networking becomes an advantage. Here, you know somebody that knows somebody, and your name is pushed forward. Very few people get to use this entry firsthand. In the context of what we're talking about, the guy who gets this opportunity walked into money or luck more often than not but could, a small percentage of the time, be about earning your way in as well.

3) The Scrapper entry- This is the side door entry or the crack in the window entry. Here, the person enters unusually through passages that are not normally used. To use this entry, you must be ready to work hard as well as smart. The scrapper leaned into the possibilities

and was willing to think outside the box, dig a little deeper to reach the destination.

You ask yourself, why wouldn't the main entry people give more thought to being the scrapper? The scrapper got in, and they were left in the cold. The answer is simple: The fear of leaving their friends, leaving the known, and leaving what was comfortable created a risk-averse situation for the main entry people.

Get on the success road and buy into the big picture because it's going to open up doors for you. It may not be today. It may not be tomorrow. It may not be in a month. It may be 12 months from now, but I've never in my lifetime seen a person I've worked with that has busted their tail and not been rewarded in some shape or fashion.

Fear of change right now in the world isn't new to us. COVID 19 is a scary thing that changed the world in less than a year. We are not new to change; we have been dealing with it on smaller scales for centuries. Think back to the last thirty years and remember how people took computers, the Walkman, cell phones, video games, and social media when they all first came out. Some people even believed that it was some kind of conspiracy to turn us all into robots and would make us dumber and numb. But today, those are some of the greatest inventions ever, and they have evolved several times after that to become better versions of the original. The opportunity to gain large amounts of knowledge at once has never been more accessible or convenient. The concept of remote work has never been more efficient. There are certainly drawbacks and disadvantages, but do they outweigh the advantages? We must understand that we are not fully replacing old things. It's not a wholesale change. These things just assimilate and integrate into each other.

Intelligent people improvise, adapt, make space in their hearts, make space within them, and improvise when moving forward.

Smile. Listen. Feel.

Strong technical skills may score you an internship or score well on a written test, but the further you get into the process, the more you realize that it's not all about what you know. It's how you apply that knowledge. If IQ was the core value in teaching, leading, coaching, etc., the personnel in all of those types of positions would look very different. It's understanding the significance of inter-personal skills and their impact on your employability status that is important. No matter how educated or talented you believe yourself to be, how you treat people ultimately tells the real story. Integrity and intentional love-based thinking are paramount.

Unpack Your Thinking; Do you believe in change? Do you believe that people remain the same, or is there a part of you that knows that we are all capable of change? Would you rather make a difference or make an impression?

Energy Audit

- *What did I put my energy toward most today?*
- *Did I put it into empathizing with others?*

- *Did I put it into getting riled up about something? Did that add value to others?*
- *Where did my energy go? Why?*
    - *Was it on a computer? Social Media? Positively towards others? Negative? Was it spent here?*

Unpack Your Thinking: Do you believe in change? Do you believe that the scars inside you stay inside you, or is there a sliver of you that believes we're capable of change? Would you rather make a difference or make an impression?

CHAPTER 7

Servant Leadership

A beautiful mind begins with a beautiful mindset

"Everybody can be great... because everybody can serve. You don't have to have a college degree to serve. You don't have to make your subject and verb agree to serve. You only need a heart full of grace. A soul generated by love." — Martin Luther King, Jr.

At the very core of leadership is service. The ability to put others' needs before your needs-a selflessness-that fuels you to want the best for those who look up to you. This is embodied in all the world's great leaders who were ready to die so that future generations might have a chance at a better life. Martin Luther King Jr, Nelson Mandela, Mahatma Gandhi, Mother Teresa, Albert Schweitzer, and others like them, both known and unknown, all had one central theme–service that translated into selflessness. As a servant leader, you're the eyes to those followers who cannot see, legs to those who cannot walk, and so on. You are what they need you to be when they need it. They are learning to skydive for the first time, and you are the instructor who tethers yourself to them. You are the airbag that erupts to prevent them from hitting their heads on the steering wheel of life. You are the handyman–always ready to repair, rebuild, replace, and unclog.

Meditate on the truth today. While principles can change over time, the truth will always be etched in stone. As discussed in Chapter Four, there are multiple routes to take when meditating. My favorite form of mediation is gratitude. I fill my cup up with gratitude, and it fuels and drives my engine. Today, fill your cup with positivity, fill it up with encouragement and kindness, with tough-minded optimism, resilience, and joy.

I watched a video one morning of a little baby belting out a deep belly gut roll laugh. With his big chubby cheeks and rolls everywhere, there was so much joy in his laughter that I immediately felt grateful. If you look in the right places, you will find reasons to be thankful. Studies show that you can't be grateful and stressed at the same time.

What does your gratitude radius look like today?

By focusing on gratitude, you will enhance the quality of every aspect of your life. It will be the catalyst for business success, in your relationships, with your teammates, and everything within your radius. Gratitude is a centerpiece to all of your projects, dreams, desires, and goals. An investment in being 1% stronger every day in the area of gratitude is an investment in you, your family, your community, and people you cross paths with every day without even knowing their names. An investment in gratitude shows that you are a big picture thinker and invest in people by design.

As is the case with all that has already been covered, gratitude has to be something you live. Simply knowing the right answer won't improve your everyday operations. You can't just talk about it. You have to be about it. It has to be something that runs in your veins, something you want almost as bad as you want to breathe. The more you practice it, the more it seeps into your veins and becomes ingrained into your culture. The more you give, the more you get. My life has steadily improved as I've learned to do good deeds. I wish I recognized the value of this earlier in my life.

I wish I would've recognized the value of this earlier in my life.

Whatever you choose as a priority, you will be motivated to make it a success. It will be obvious to everyone around you, and they will assimilate the same culture. Life isn't about finding yourself but rather about creating yourself and shaping the lifestyle you wish to lead. Genetics may give you some tools to begin your journey, but your decision to lead a life serving thanks to your opportunities and giving gratitude to the blessings around you will define you.

"*A master in the art of living draws no sharp distinction between his work and his play; his labor and his leisure; his mind and his body; his education and his recreation. He hardly knows which is which. He simply pursues his vision of excellence through whatever he is doing, and leaves others to determine whether he is working or playing. To himself, he always appears to be doing both.*"

–Minister Lawrence Pearsall Jacks

Long-distance runner Marios Giannakou, a Greek athlete, demonstrated a heartwarming act of servanthood when he crossed paths with Eleftheria Tosiou. Mario had climbed the legendary Mount Olympus at least a dozen times, while Eleftheria, a twenty-two-year-old lady with a disability, had not, due to her physical circumstances. Mario proved that heroes aren't only something you read about in legendary, mythical stories as he decided to make Eleftheria the first person with a disability to reach the top of Mount Olympus, as that was her dream. Giannakou said he wanted to try to get up there with her to the highest peak in Greece, carrying her on his back, and that's exactly what he did. He made a specially modified backpack for Eleftheria and climbed ten hours with an eight-man crew before reaching the top. He was able to accomplish something, not only for himself but for somebody else, the ultimate double win.

Marios Giannakou, a Greek athlete, with Eleftheria Tosiou

Who will you piggyback on the road to success today?

When your focus is that of a servant leader, you recognize that your job isn't about you—it's about fostering support, coaching up, and lifting up the people around you. You wish for dynamic success in their everyday work, constant growth. You want to create the greatest growth hackers in the world within your organization and treat them not only as if they're your equal but as individuals you serve. You exist to create the best versions of you and those around you. This is true servant leadership.

Below are five achievable Calls to Action for servant leadership:

- Discover the stressors in the lives of those you work with. What are the root causes for their frustration and high stress levels? It could be wide-ranging. Staying late, long commutes stuck in traffic, personality conflicts, or simply unfamiliarity with new programs and or personnel. Serve them by finding ways to reduce the stress in their lives.

- A small acknowledgment can go far, not only in serving the people you work with but in setting the standard for how people should be treated. Others nearby observing your acts of gratitude could potentially create a gratitude revolution, shaping the culture you desire to be a part of. When others see the leader showing appreciation with something as simple as a handshake, a personal thank you, a small note, or perhaps even complimenting another person in a coffee shop; it will have a great impact. Speaking from your heart and leaving footprints for others to follow in your work leaves a lasting imprint in others' lives.

- You work with them; they do not work for you. Treat them as human beings, as more than just a spot on the roster or a title. Winners can juggle relationships that teeter along the lines of business and personal life while still garnering respect in the most difficult circumstances.

- Be intentional in learning the moments that matter in the lives of the people around you. Find out about those big moments—"firsts" are always big. Learn about their first day on the job, first house, the first day of anything—and do something showing them you value that experience. Serve those around you with empathy and caring measures. When you find weaknesses within them, look for ways to help them become stronger, observe to know what is standing in between them and their best self, and make sure your motive is bordered with love.

Unpack Your Thinking: What are some ways you can help relieve them of stress and help build them up?

BEST SELF-UNIFORM

What kind of uniform are you wearing today specifically?

Are you wearing your uniform upside down? Do you have your priorities reversed? Are you keeping score of the wrong things? If so, you can reverse engineer your core values and reprioritize them. You have that gift!

Are you wearing it backward, tracking life with the wrong lens? If so, the beautiful thing is that self-awareness is a habit we can cultivate. Do you have a friend or colleague wearing it backward? Remember that you're only one conversation away from changing not only your life but those around you.

Are you wearing someone else's uniform? You were not brought into this world to be just a character in someone else's story. You are unique and endowed with a lot to add to the world.

What if I told you that being a great listener is part of that uniform? What if I told you that you don't have to be knowledgeable to be a great listener? You just have to be available. You've got to be slow to speak, and you've got to be quick to listen.

You've got to be slow to speak, and you've got to be quick to listen.

Ideas to help you and your team of people wear the best self-uniform, creating space for a life of servanthood.

1.) Make the present your priority. Win this day. Enjoy the process. The process isn't always straightforward.

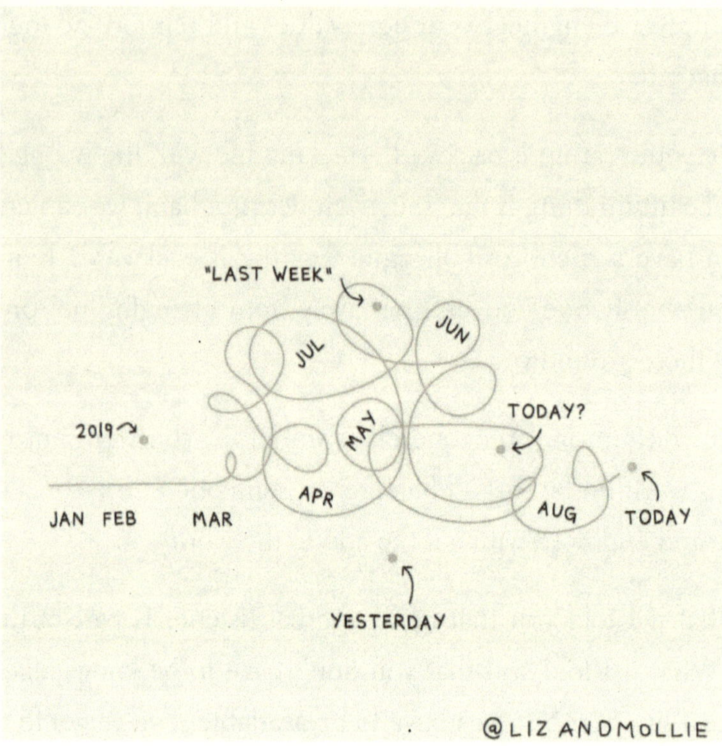

2) The success road is not a destination. Success is the road, and the road has a way of moving all over the place. Winning today gives us our best shot at being our best self tomorrow. While we want to be a big picture guy, what the big picture needs out of us is to be present and be where our feet are. So many people have a permanent telescope lens and end up wandering aimlessly. We need to mix in the microscope lens to be efficient with the tasks in front of us.

3) Are you riding on the train of positivity? Are you looking to get 1% better every day? Remember that the one percent better version of you every day, for 365, that's going to be a 37% increase in your happiness. That sounds like a pretty good deal!

4) Be fearless. Because on the other side of fear is fulfillment. Don't get hung up on the possibility of failure. Focus instead on how great it's going to feel when you get there. Don't let fear be a major factor of consideration on your journey. It is really just a figment of your imagination.

Should fear really be a factor for you?

5) Be a great communicator. Poor communication is not only the biggest deal killer in business but also in relationships. When you don't know when, where, and how to speak, you will give room for people to start making up their own ideas and assumptions about you. Usually, they will be negative. Negativity easily seeps into empty spaces, so be careful not to leave your communication vault empty.

6) Develop yourself. Read books, listen to podcasts, and be intentional with gaining new knowledge. Being a lifelong learner is one of the best ways to invest in yourself. You may not know this, but it is a selfish move not to develop yourself. It is selfish to your circle, to your family, and all those whose lives are tied to yours in one way or the other. Servanthood is a choice. A choice that can determine the legacy you leave in others.

7) Lastly, continuous investment, not only in you but in your relationships. Those that play together stay together. That lesson carries over to every relationship in your life.

Servanthood is a choice. A choice that can determine the legacy you leave in others.

CHAPTER 8

Avoiding the Prison Sentence

How do you prime your brain for everyday growth?

In the movie *Forrest Gump*, a young boy by the name of Forrest has cognitive challenges. After struggling with leg issues as a child, he discarded his leg braces and went to college to play football, becoming a fan favorite. His childhood friend, Jenny, stood up for him throughout their lives. Forrest joins the army, and his friend, Bubba, persuades him to go to the shrimp business when the war is over. Sadly, Bubba is killed. Despite his perceived disadvantages, Forrest became a hero in a number of areas. He would go on to be married to his childhood friend, Jenny, and together they'd have a child. Forest could have led a life where he had become a prison of his own making. He could have had built-in excuses. In this world where everybody puts up barriers to their true self and is always trying to be something or someone other than who they really are, it is easy to bury yourself with pity. Don't fall for it. Just as Forrest did, write your own story and create a plot with your own twist!

The world is full of emotional, physical, and mental prisons. You need to take your time and do some introspection, find out the prison you are in, and begin the process of freeing yourself. Let nothing be able to hold you hostage. Sometimes even as we journey on the road to success, we can become prisoners to that journey. A person can become so hung up on the prospect of success. They begin to build prison walls around themselves without knowing it.

Does the decision you're about to make expand your growth?

Does the decision you're about to make expand your growth, or does it box you in with a limited ceiling surrounded by perceived thick walls? Chasing growth on the success road is similar to chasing the skyline. You'll never reach it, but the journey will be amazing as you will watch growth unfold right in front of your eyes. Good mentors, teachers, parents always say that seeing their pupil or child develop into a better version of themselves may be the most rewarding thing they have experienced in their lives. The most promising route to the equivalent of a lifetime personal development prison sentence is to have a fixed mindset. With this, you have a limited capacity for growth, limited space for freedom within you, and small windows of opportunity for fulfillment comparatively. The fastest and most efficient path to priming your brain for every day growth is an investment not only in yourself but in the relationships of those you cross paths with.

MAKERS vs. TAKERS

On one side of life are Makers, and on the other side are Takers.

- Makers are those people who are more interested in long-lasting results than in immediate gratification. They are more concerned with creating opportunities for others' betterment than generating wealth for themselves. They are not concerned about praises from people or worldly recognition. They take pride instead in the legacy they are leaving behind. For you to be a winner and champion in life, you must be a maker, someone who is unselfish enough to create opportunities for others without hesitation. Makers are remembered even after they are gone. Songs are sung about them, and people are greatly inspired by them. They are not the majority, but their impact is felt in places they have never been. Makers are trailblazers, risk-takers with a strong culture of gratitude, love, and empathy. Be a maker today!

- Takers, on the other hand, care for only the now and their own wellbeing. They have little desire to leave any lasting effect on the world, and they do not mind crushing others to get what they want. The process does not concern them. They are all about the outcome and how it favors them. They do not put their resources into anything unless it benefits them, and their culture is that of selfishness, shortcuts, and instant gratification. You're not going to see the person holding doors open, picking up another person's paperwork that fell on the floor. They're not going to be overly concerned about the well-being of the community, etc.

Talent vs. TalentED

The difference between talent and talented is talented has an "ed" on the end. "ED" stands for exceptionally different. You want to be exceptionally different. You don't want to be like everybody else. You don't want to blend in. If you're an athlete and they throw on the tape, you want to jump off the screen. If you're interviewing for a job, you want to stand out from the last guy. You want to be different, exceptionally different–"ED." You must constantly remind yourself that being your best self is not chance; it is choice.

Being your best self is not chance; it is a choice.

Talented people think and act differently. When people interact with them, it is obvious that they are not like everybody else. Talented people are wired to compete every day in life. They compete! The process might differ, but the aim is always the same: improving their previous best self. You're not competing against life but your previous best self. The talentED shape a talent code that has granted them trust from others. Trust is a more important concept than success because trust is the foundation of great relationships. While we can't predict whether or not we will gain someone's trust, we can do our best to make sure that we live a life of real talk and full of integrity.

Truth is also a very important concept in life. Talented individuals do not take the truth lightly. They live the truth, they learn the truth, and they let the truth guide them. Seeking out the truth can take some vigilance and perseverance, but when you willingly put in the time and effort, you are rewiring yourself for the talentED mindset.

Positive Pinpointing

The most effective form of helping others grow is positive pinpointing. It's huge for building relationships. It is the true power grid in life and encourages people to repeat behavior patterns that help them. They may not have accomplished the desired result, but if they have the desired behavior and/or pattern, they should repeat them and build on them to have a future desired result. Every time someone performs a desired behavior, you've got to make a big deal out of it. You've got to compliment them. This does not only pertain to teachers, coaches, and leaders of massive organizations. This is a universal necessity for growth in any capacity.

Less Tik, more Talk

The talentED growth-minded individuals understand that life is less about the tick and more about the talk. We need to engage with people, and we've got to get people engaged. To make this happen, you have to speak the truth, have to be authentic, and you'll want to be a love-tough advocate for others. When people see that you serve them, they'll open up new doors to stronger relationships. Remember the 90% rule of communication. Ninety perfect of all relationships fail because of communication, or lack thereof. You must establish emotional connections. As I have stated many times in this book, relationships are the strongest currency you have. It's the currency that never goes bankrupt. Relationships could begin anywhere and go on for years.

I met my wife when she was a survey girl, working for Pepsi at a youth baseball tournament. I mean, what are the odds of that?

Relevance

I use myself as an example, and I'm not proud of this at all. But for the sake of teaching and transparency, I probably didn't read a full book until my third year of college. It is an embarrassing truth, and I sometimes wish it wasn't a part of my story. In reflection, my biggest issue was that I didn't see the cause behind most of my schooling despite knowing the benefits. I was a good kid. I knew I needed to do my schoolwork, but I didn't see the need or understand the cause. When you know the cause and tie it in with purpose and motivation, it produces a more emotional investment, and when there's an emotional investment, you will give your best effort.

The only measurement tool worth following is growth percentage. Write that down.

The only measurement tool worth following, whether in business, life, sport, or relationships, is the growth percentage. When I compete, I always want to out improve. That should be your goal. It's not a number. Most stats are totally overrated. Some are relevant, but the one thing you should be concentrating on is being better than what is already available. If you're comparing yourself to another business, *I want to out improve you*, or maybe you're just speaking to your previous best self. I *want to out improve you.* The end result is a stronger currency. Relationship capital, social capital, financial capital, the entire spectrum of capital is strengthened.

It's not win or lose; it's win or *learn.* The talentED understand this. The talented know how to hire. I'm sure CEOs and a lot of other people in a position of hiring are reading this right now. What is it you're looking for in a hire? The talentED ones understand that businesses are built from the inside out, and that great individuals are built from the inside out. You should be more concerned with how they treat others. You want scrappers, you want grinders, you want people with grit and tenacity.

While You Were Sleeping

I once watched a movie titled *Why You Were Sleeping*, starring Sandra Bullock. It told a story of a girl who saved a guy on a train but the guy, named Peter, ends up in a coma. The family thinks she is his fiancé. While he's in the coma, they all get to know and like her and grow very close. Later down the line, Peter finally wakes up and has no idea who she is. This leads them to a "get to know you" conversation. In it, Peter begins to speak of Lucy's (Sandra Bullock) heroism. Peter then says, "I don't think I've done anything truly heroic my whole life."

Lucy replies, "You give your seat up every day on the train."

Peter answers, "Well, that's not heroic."

But Sandra Bullock's character, Lucy, replies, "It is to the person who sits in it. It always gave me something to look forward to."

My point here is that it takes no special ability to be kind, to have honor, to do right. YOU are a perfect candidate. YOU can do this today. YOU can do this right now. The double win is ready, willing, and waiting to be yours.

It takes no special ability to be kind.

Winners Delight

True winners get excited about others winning. They're happy when other people get to experience the euphoria of success. True winners are healthy competitors; they engage only in competition that helps them become the best version of themselves. Competition should help us grow into the best version of ourselves and be welcomed with open arms. It forces you to stretch your limits. It forces you to embrace struggle. These days, it has become increasingly hard to find people who are happy for others' success. People who understand that they didn't receive the medal or award and have their names shouted for all to hear know they are not failures. Apart from the winning or losing part, the competition process itself helps change and better our approach to life. We discover skills that we didn't know we had. We are able to gauge our ability to work under pressure and how much of a team player or lone wolf we are. Instead of other people's wins getting under your skin, intentionally congratulate them and let it encourage you to do better. There is enough room in this world for all of us.

Conclusion

You must rule your world. There is so much out there for the taking that is calling your name. You are not defined by the statutes and principles of this world but by those you set for yourself. As you go on your journey through life, take others along. Clean tears and replace them with laughter. Give gifts that no amount of money can buy. Commit yourself to building a world where people feel safe and good enough. Let your life be a living example of what greatness looks like when it is fully embodied. In your small circle or large organization, let your life be an encouragement. You are not cut from the same cloth as everyone else. You have read up to this moment because you have a passion for change. Let the words in this book guide you on your journey. Share the principles with those who you wish to journey alongside you. Strive to leave a legacy that will inspire greatness in others. There is no greater reward than being a blessing to those whose paths cross yours in this journey of life.

Works Cited

Burchard, Brendon. High Performance Habits. Hay House, 2017.

Collins, Jim. Good to Great. Harper Business, 2001.

Dorfman, Harvey A., and Karl Kuehl. The Mental Game of Baseball: A Guide to Peak Performance. Taylor Trade Publishing, 2017.

Gable, Kirkland. Winner's Way. Star Cloud Press, 2009.

Heath, Chip, and Dan Heath. Made to Stick: Why Some Ideas Survive, and Others Die. Woonjing ThinkBig Co., 2007.

Jaeger, Alan. Mental Skills Must Be Regularly.

Janssen, Jeff, and Dave Brandon. How to Build and Sustain a Championship Culture: Your 10-Step Blueprint to Build a Winning Culture of Commitment, Accountability, and Ownership. Winning the Mental Game, 2015.

Lewis, Robert. Winning at Work & Home: Authentic Manhood. LifeWay Press, 2006.

Maxwell, John C. How Successful People Think: Change Your Thinking, Change Your Life. Center Street, 2016.

Maxwell, John C. The 17 Essential Qualities of a Team Player: Becoming the Kind of Person Every Team Wants. Nelson Business, 2007.

Maxwell, John C. Winning with People. Jaico Publishing House, 2012.

McDougall, Christopher. Born to Run: the Rise of Ultra-Running and the Super-Athlete Tribe. Profile, 2008.

Morris, Thomas V. The Art of Achievement: Mastering the 7 Cs of Success in Business and Life. Andrews McMeel Pub., 2002.

Nelson, Kurt, Ph.D. How to avoid 10 of the most common Leadership Blind Spots.

Ravizza, Ken, and Tom Hanson. Heads-up Baseball: Playing the Game One Pitch at a Time. McGraw-Hill, 1995.

Robinett, Judy. How to Be a Power Connector: the 5 50 100 Rule for Turning Your Business Network into Profits. McGraw-Hill Education, 2014.

Nichols, Lisa. "Motivating the Masses." *Motivating The Masses*, Motivating The Masses, https://motivatingthemasses.com/about/lisa-nichols/

Goal Setting Worksheet

Instructions: Record as many goals as you feel necessary. Each one should be meaningful and palatable to you. Take time to research issues you need to with colleagues, coaches, friends, teammates, etc. When you finish, you should see some logic from the bottom to the top of the page. If you succeed in your daily and weekly goals, you will likely meet your single-performance goals; meeting these goals should allow you to meet your yearly goals, which, if done, should allow you to meet your lifetime goals.

My Performance-Specific Goals

Name______________________________ Date Recorded_____________

My lifetime goals are to:

My goals for the next 90 days are:

In each performance, I would like to achieve influence and my goals by:

Each week, my goals are to:

Day to day, my goals are to:

Success Formula for Handling Adversity

It's not experience that matters; it's what you do with the experiences you have.

Repeat what works; change the systems that don't.

Ask yourself:

1. What was I trying to do? (Your answer should be controllable)
2. What did I do well?
3. Why?
4. What did I learn?

Example (Baseball):

1. What was I trying to do? (Your answer should be controllable)
Let the ball travel to hit the ball, hit the ball hard where it was pitched

2. How did it go?
Well. I hit a fly ball hard to Right Field

3. Why?
Because I saw it well, arrived on time, and put my best swing on it.

4. What do I want to do the next time I'm in a similar situation?
The same thing.

Take Away

- Have a short-term memory. Forgive and Forget
- You are not perfect. Look forward to the struggles. It's what makes us stronger.
- Poor behavior/adjustments are a common result of poor or nonuse of the brain. Without analysis, no adjustment can be made. Are you a problem solver or a problem dweller? Are you going to do something about it, or are you going to find a mentality that is weak, soft and a dead end? If it is to be, it is up to me.

10 Key Moves to Making you a stronger and tougher minded individual

Simply fill in your key moves at any point during your reading. Let these be your reminders.

10 Key Moves-A Work in Progress
1.
2.
3.
4.
5.
6.
7.
8.
9.
10.

THANK YOU FOR READING MY BOOK!

DOWNLOAD YOUR FREE GIFTS

Read This First

Just to say thanks for buying and reading my book, I would like to give you a 100% bonus gift for FREE, no strings attached!

To Download Now, Visit:
www.BradDaltonGroup.com/freegift

I appreciate your interest in my book, and I value your feedback as it helps me improve future versions of this book. I would appreciate it if you could leave your invaluable review on Amazon.com with your feedback. Thank you!

www.ingramcontent.com/pod-product-compliance
Lightning Source LLC
LaVergne TN
LVHW051001080826
845145LV00009B/2401

* 9 7 8 1 7 3 6 5 4 9 1 4 8 *